# The History of Accounting

This is a volume in the Arno Press collection

# The History of Accounting



*See last pages of this volume for a complete list of titles*

# THE NATURAL BUSINESS YEAR

## AND THIRTEEN OTHER THEMES

BY

ELIJAH WATT SELLS

ARNO PRESS

A New York Times Company

New York — 1976

Editorial Supervision: SHEILA MEHLMAN

Reprint Edition 1976 by Arno Press Inc.

Reprinted from a copy in The American Institute
of Certified Public Accountants Library

THE HISTORY OF ACCOUNTING
ISBN for complete set: 0-405-07540-5
See last pages of this volume for titles.

Manufactured in the United States of America

**Library of Congress Cataloging in Publication Data**

Sells, Elijah Watt, 1858-1924.
The natural business year, and thirteen other themes.

(The History of accounting)
Reprint of the ed. published by A. W. Shaw Co., Chicago.
1. Accounting--Addresses, essays, lectures.
2. Business--Addresses, essays, lectures. I. Title.
II. Series.
HF5616.U5S4 1976 657 75-18484
ISBN 0-405-07566-9

# THE NATURAL BUSINESS YEAR

## AND THIRTEEN OTHER THEMES

© Underwood & Underwood

ELIJAH WATT SELLS

March 1, 1858 — March 19, 1924

# THE NATURAL BUSINESS YEAR

## AND THIRTEEN OTHER THEMES

BY

ELIJAH WATT SELLS
M.A. (Hon.) D.C.S (Hon.) C.P.A.

CHICAGO & NEW YORK
A. W. SHAW COMPANY
LONDON, A. W. SHAW AND COMPANY, LIMITED
1924

PRINTED IN THE UNITED STATES OF AMERICA

# FOREWORD

*By* William George Jordan

The youngest of all the professions in America is accountancy. The recency of its history is evident when we realize that practically its complete story is comprised within the brief span of the life of one man. Before that, accounting was little more than a glorified bookkeeping, with auditing on a small scale. Its greatest strides have been within the past quarter-century. Reviewing the great events of his time, and paraphrasing the words of a famous statesman, Elijah Watt Sells might modestly have said of the profession in America: "All of which I saw, and in much of which I had some part."

Mr. Sells was born in Muscatine, Iowa, on March 1, 1858. His father, Elijah Sells, held many state and Government offices, among which were those of Secretary of the State of Iowa, Third Auditor of the Treasury, and Auditor of the Treasury Department under President Lincoln. His mother was Isabel Watt Sells.

It was in the public schools of Iowa that young Elijah received his earliest education, after which he went to Baker University, at Baldwin, Kansas. He had a strong yearning early in life to make his own way in the world, and strove always to that end.

It is strange in life that the memories which give us the most pleasure, which are always accompanied by a half-smile and a warm glow as we recall them, are not our triumphs, but our struggles; not the golden goals of achievement, but the lonely pathways of effort. Perhaps it is all some subtle illusion of the perspective of memory.

Mr. Sells had a number of these to look back on with pleasure, for the golden spoon was absent from his layette. During his school vacations he worked for a country expressman delivering goods from a wagon to consignees. Later, he was general utility helper around a drug store, selling cigars and newspapers. Then he served time as a messenger in a telegraph office, learned to be a "plug" operator, and something about the operation of a railway station. Following this he went to Gardiner, Kansas, and began to acquire his knowledge of railroads as agent and telegraph operator, which included such work as sweeping and cleaning round the station, handling trunks, and other work of similar importance. He was also a ticket agent, express agent, porter, and a number of other things. Though he was only a boy of 16, he did his work admirably, and was polite and popular. He had, however, one failing—his accounting was bad; he could never make his records come out right. The visiting official of the road complimented him on the manner in which he handled the station, but gave him a gentle reprimand on the inaccuracies of his accounts. Piqued at the reproof, the young station agent vowed that never would such a thing be said to him again. And it never was.

On his transfer shortly afterward to a better post in the station at Baldwin, Kansas, after a year of service another visiting official showed that Mr. Sells had not made a single mistake in his handling of 12 months of business. Promoted to a position in the railroad general office at Kansas City, Missouri, he began as office helper to check way-bills. The man above him leaving, he volunteered to do the work of both. He accomplished this easily and successfully, and began to be recognized as apt in figures. He became general bookkeeper, and was often sent to other places on the road to straighten out tangles in accounting. Then he was tranferred to Dubuque, Iowa, as bookkeeper, cashier, and paymaster of a railroad.

Shortly after this he went west to become chief clerk to the comptroller of the Oregon Railway and Navigation Company and the Oregon Improvement Company, later becoming auditor of the Oregon Improvement Company and its allied interests. Afterwards he was appointed assistant comptroller of the Kansas City, Fort Scott and Memphis Railway, at Kansas City, where he hád spent his earlier years, and then secretary and auditor of the Colorado Midland Railway; afterwards with the Atchison, Topeka and Santa Fe. During this period, and immediately following, he was frequently engaged on special accounting matters, and sometimes by other corporations to make special examinations of their accounts and to introduce new accounting systems, work much in the nature of public accounting as we know it today. On two occasions he made trips to New York for conferences relative to entering the public accounting field.

The success of Mr. Sells was no matter of luck or favoritism. He earned every advance by his ability, loyalty, and faithful service, never questioning or cavilling about the pay he received, never asking for a raise. He was picked out for promotion because he stood out from his fellows by the superiority of his work. The quality of his mind, as discerned by those who knew him in manhood, was simply the fine flowering of his characteristics as a boy. Just as the veining of a leaf suggests in miniature the branching of the tree, so the youth foreshadowed the man.

If we could submit a man's mental and moral characteristics to some kind of psychic analysis as a chemist does with some substance in his laboratory, we could reduce the whole man to certain elemental qualities that constitute him, that make him what he is. His success or failure would then be seen not as incidental or accidental, but inevitable. It is as the summation of a given column of figures is foreordained in the logic of mathematics.

If one might venture to submit Mr. Sells to such a process, the resultant elements would, in part at least, read like this: Broadness of mind and sympathy, vision, a keen analytic reasoning process sure of its facts and rapid and safe in its decisions, initiative, resourcefulness, thoroughness, cool calmness, respect for the opinions of others but courage in his own, untiring industry, rare kindliness and generosity, all tempered and inspired by a high sense of humor and justice.

It was in 1893 that Mr. Sells' great opportunity came. It was one for which his abilities specially fitted him; he was ready, for he had been unconsciously training himself to handle a big work in his years of faithful performance of every task that he undertook.

In March, 1893, a Joint Commission of the Fifty-third Congress was appointed to "inquire into and examine the status of the laws organizing the executive departments, bureaus, divisions, and other Government establishments at the capital; the rules, regulations, and methods for the conduct of the same; the time and attention devoted to the operations thereof by the persons employed therein and the grade of efficiency of all such employees; whether any modification of these laws can be made to secure greater efficiency and economy, and whether a reduction in the number or compensation of the persons authorized to be employees in the state executive departments or bureaus can be made without injury to the public service."

The commission was composed of Alexander M. Dockery, chairman; James D. Richardson, and Nelson Dingley, Jr., members on the part of the House of Representatives; F. M. Cockrell, James K. Jones, and S. M. Cullen, members on the part of the Senate.

The commission was generally known as the "Dockery Commission."

The technical phrasing of the work outlined for the commission does not quite do justice to its scope and the real reason. Put in plain, unvarnished English, it meant that the Government methods of handling business were clumsy and antiquated; they represented a survival of methods good enough when the country was in its boyhood, a little group of states bordering on the Atlantic. The area of the nation's activities was then small as compared with its spread to the Pacific; population, revenue, influence, problems, resources, needs had become colossal. The old methods had been modified, it is true, added to and somehow brought into harmony with newer needs, but it had been done in a haphazard, unscientific way. Great business corporations, like our railways and trusts, had moved with the times; the Government had not.

The years had brought endless red tape which threw its delaying and entangling lengths into the machinery; there was duplication of effort, cumbersome, outworn systems, barnacles of unnecessary officeholders, waste of money, time and effort, useless records carefully kept and meticulously counter-checked, square pegs wobbling in round holes, precedent standing in the way of progress. These and a dozen other economic and business diseases were sapping the vitality of the departments. They all needed a sanitary housecleaning from the standpoint of accounting; the old, worn-out and useless methods to be discarded, like rubbish cleared out of an attic, and new, wise, sane, practical and safe, up-to-date methods to take their place. The commission members believed in this; they were pledged to put it through; the press and public, except those office-holders who feared to be ousted, were in hearty sympathy and gave the movement their cordial support. The commissioners knew just what they wanted, and they got results far beyond their dreams, because they went about it in the right way, and because they were singularly fortunate in their choice of the men to carry on the work.

Under the act authorizing the commission, provision was made for the employment of not to exceed three experts to render such assistance as the commission might require. This in itself was an innovation. Prior to this, there had been some weak, ineffective attempts to improve the business conduct of the departments, but it had been by investigations of men on the inside, themselves under the spell of the old traditions, hampered by fear or by favoritism, not daring to make radical suggestions or recommendations, even had they been able to do so.

It was a stroke of inspiration, natural though it seems, to place the work in the hands of outsiders; men who could view the problems with a fresh eye; men trained to systematic study, rapidly mobilizing their facts and calmly considering them carefully before pronouncing judgment; men long familiar with the best methods of the great corporations; experts in accounting, unhampered by affiliations or patronage, with no fear but that of not doing their best.

It was no easy task to find the very men in all the country to conduct this great work which one of the leading newspapers compared to that stupendous feat in mythology, the cleaning up of the Augean stables that had not known mop or broom or spade or hose for 40 years. The commission spent over a month in making its selection. The two men finally chosen were Charles Waldo Haskins, of New York, and Elijah Watt Sells, of Chicago.

These men had never before seen each other, but at their first meeting in Washington were so strongly attracted, one to the other, that there began immediately a rare, vital friendship and a business relation that remained unbroken till the hand of death removed Mr. Haskins 10 years later. It was one of the romances of our prosaic business world that joined and held together these two men in the bonds of a common friendship, loyalty, and affection. Both men of unusual gifts and powers, standing at the head of their profession, they were unlike in characteristics and in temperament, but the fine, sturdy virtues were common to both. They mutually supplemented each other and followed the same ideals; lived in accord with the same vision; held the same high standards, and both loved with equal rare zeal their profession, together seeking to advance it with the loyalty and devotion of a sacred mission.

They started in to work in June, 1893, and for over a year and a half, or until March, 1895, labored tirelessly together. The full story of what they accomplished and how they did it is one of great human interest in all its details and of greater interest from its economic and business results, but it is too long to chronicle in this brief sketch of Mr. Sells and his work.

Their labors were voluminous and exacting. They necessitated close contact not only with members of the commission, but with various Government officials. It required not only signal ability as accountants, but tact and diplomacy in the handling of men. It called not only for patience and close application, but unswerving adherence to the purpose of the investigation. It resulted in many revisions in the accounting system and in facilitating the conduct of the business of government in many ways. The commission accomplished all it set out to do, and all that could be done in the time at its disposal. The annual saving of more than $600,000 was the mere outward symbol of the improved health and tonic vitality given to the whole service.

The Hon. Redfield Proctor, of Vermont, spoke in the United States Senate on July 15, 1895, in highest terms of praise of the work of the experts, and on the completion of their labors Alexander M. Dockery tendered them an engrossed testimonial of appreciation on behalf of the Joint Commission, of which he was chairman.

It was inevitable that the two co-workers should go into partnership. This they did on March 4, 1895, opening an office at Number 2 Nassau Street, New York. The offices were removed, however, on May 1, 1896, to the Johnston Building, 30 Broad Street, in which the firm of Haskins & Sells was one of the first tenants, and where it has since continuously maintained an office.

Among the firm's first engagements, in April, 1895, was an examination of the methods of accounting at Vassar College, an engagement which came from Mr. S. D. Coykendall, a stranger to both at that time. Either Mr. Coykendall or his son has been ever since a client of the firm.

The engagements which followed embraced services for the Government, states, municipalities, insurance companies, banks and trust companies, street and steam railways, mercantile and industrial organizations of every description. The services of the firm, on account of the extensive railroad experience of the founders, were in large demand by the leading railway corporations. During the period of these early engagements, the firm received considerable publicity through the discovery of many serious irregularities in the accounts of the auditor of one of the southern railroads and his conviction on their testimony furnished at the trial.

The growing practice in the Middle West led to the opening of an office in the Marquette Building in Chicago, on December 1, 1900. The importance of this step was apparent when the City of Chicago engagement soon followed. On June 24, 1901, the City Council of Chicago passed an order authorizing the mayor, comptroller, and chairman of the committee on finance to engage a firm of accountants to introduce and supervise a uniform system of accounting and auditing in all the departments of the city government. The committee entered into an agreement with the firm of Haskins & Sells. The work was prosecuted vigorously during the succeeding months and a report submitted in November, 1901. The city council passed an ordinance in December adopting the system. It was inaugurated January 1, 1902.

The new system achieved great success. It not only effected economies during the first year of operation amounting to $72,630, but resulted in an increase of $436,770.46 in miscellaneous revenues. The city comptroller in his first report issued under the new system said: "It is now evident that the system has proved an advantage to the city government; that it has improved the efficiency of individual employees and prompted an intelligent and interested direction of their efforts by department heads."

The year 1901 saw the first evidence of international expansion. Under date of April 10, 1901, the firm announced the opening of an office at 30 Coleman Street, London, E. C. Many American firms and companies doing business abroad recognized the advantages of retaining American accountants and availed themselves of the opportunity.

In January, 1902, the firm opened an office in St. Louis in connection with its service in handling the accounts of street railways and other matters. Thereafter one new office speedily followed another, until today the firm is represented in 32 cities, and consists of 25 partners. It has outgrown the limits of this country and become an international institution, known and respected the world over.

In the spring of 1905 there was much concern in New York over the administration of the three leading insurance companies. Investigations were made not only by the state insurance department, but by the insurance companies themselves. Public accountants were in each instance retained to examine into the financial affairs and report. Two firms of accountants were selected in each case to collaborate. Haskins & Sells was engaged in all three of the cases, working in conjunction with Price, Waterhouse and Company on two of the companies and with Deloitte, Plender, Griffiths and Company on the third company. Two of the engagements involved lengthy investigations and voluminous reports resulting in rather complete reorganization of the respective accounting systems. In the third case the conditions revealed less necessity for a thorough investigation. These engagements served probably to bring the firm into the public eye as much as anything in its history.

Many corporations, as they grow from humble beginnings to great power and influence, become institutionalized; one feels they are huge business mechanisms; there is increased efficiency but decreased personality; everything is reduced to such processes of system and mechanical working that the human equation is at a minimum. Not so with Haskins & Sells; efficiency and personality have grown side by side, each reenforcing the other. So well perfected was the organization that the severe shock and the sense of deep loss incident to the death of Mr. Haskins in January, 1903, were weathered in safety. There was a brief period of financial stress and strain, caused by the withdrawal of part of the partnership funds, but this was all wisely adjusted.

In all the work of Mr. Haskins in organizing the founding of the School of Commerce, Accounts, and Finance at the University of New York, Mr. Sells was a close confident, adviser, and cooperator. In this, and in other big movements in the interest of their profession, they were in such perfect mental accord and sustained by high principles and ideals so much the same that the barest suggestion of one as rapidly was clarified and enlarged by the other and it was often difficult to say to which of them the real credit for any idea or plan was due. It did not matter any way, for neither cared.

New York University, in 1916, conferred upon Mr. Sells and the late Mr. Jacob Schiff the honorary degree of Doctor of Commercial Science. Dr. George Alexander, Acting Chancellor, in conferring the degree on Mr. Sells, said: "Elijah Watt Sells—for preeminence in a department of human effort in which the prime essentials are accuracy and truth; for the prevision which prompted you to secure for accountancy academic recognition; for distinguished service rendered to local governments, and especially to the Government of the United States, both at home and abroad—I confer upon you, by authority of New York University, the degree of Doctor of Commercial Science."

This degree was a new one and had been conferred by New York University on but one previous occasion. It is a special honor which has been since awarded very sparingly for signal service in the world of commerce and business. In all, less than a dozen men have done such big and outstanding work for commercial education and governments through their initiative and original lines to render their service conspicuous enough to win the coveted honor. Among these are Mr. Charles M. Schwab and Mr. John Pierpont Morgan. Baker University, in 1909, conferred on Mr. Sells the honorary degree of Master of Arts. New York University appointed him to an honorary professorship in the early years of the School of Commerce, Accounts, and Finance.

In 1906 and 1907 Mr. Sells was elected president of the American Association of Public Accountants. In 1908 he was engaged to investigate the financial system of the Philippine Islands, under Governor-General Forbes, and in connection with this work made a trip around the globe. In the organization of the American Institute of Accountants and in the creation of the endowment fund of the Institute, Mr. Sells was an active, inspiring force. The purpose of the fund was to afford a means of collecting and disseminating information relative to accounting and accountancy. He served for seven years as a member of the Institute Council, on the executive committee, and as chairman of the budget committee, retiring only recently at his own request.

Mr. Sells was married in 1884 to Mabel Graves, who died in February, 1922, and had two children, Mrs. Arthur H. Carter and Mrs. LeRoy D. McMorris.

The scope of the valuable papers collected in this volume, entitled "The Natural Business Year and Thirteen Other Themes" or "Some Themes in Accountancy," is not necessary here to discuss, as they are reviewed by an able, critical mind, more adequate than mine to do them justice. Mr. Sells had a long, honored career, inextricably interwoven with the rise and development of accountancy in America, and the story of either the man or the profession is incomplete without that of the other.

# PREFACE

It is not inappropriate, apparently, in prefacing a symposium such as this book contains to say something of the author in addition to commenting on the essays. Such a procedure is perhaps more in order in this case since during the process of arranging for publication the author passed to the Great Beyond. Mr. Sells died on March 19, 1924, at the age of sixty-six.

Any note of criticism which may have been sounded in these papers should not be misconstrued. The author of the papers was not an iconoclast. He was not a radical. His motive in criticising was a desire to arouse public and business consciousness without aspiring to leadership or attracting to himself attention which might redound to his personal benefit.

Modest in the extreme, unassuming in attitude, Mr. Sells possessed an unusual genius for seeing things fairly and clearly, going straight to causes, and deciding on appropriate action. His early experience with the Federal Government and his years of contact with business enterprises gave him an insight into the problems of the country, economic, financial, and political, which he utilized to advantage in discussing the subjects about which he essayed to write from time to time. Naturally an accountant rather than a writer, he frequently complained of difficulty in expressing his thoughts. Possessed of whatever complex it is which produces stage-fright, he frequently experienced difficulty in speaking before even moderate-sized gatherings, and refused on many occasions to appear before large audiences when what he might have had to say would have been received with interest and enthusiasm.

The ideas and thoughts expressed in his articles were suggested to him in various ways. For example, the paper on "Corporate Management," as mentioned on page 157, grew out of an interview with the London correspondent of the *New York Times* on the occasion of one of Mr. Sells' visits to London when, at the Hotel Savoy, he was approached for an interview on American business conditions. The development of the article was conceived while, as Mr. Sells on one occasion expressed it, he was "stumbling around in the woods" near his farm. Much of the other material was the result of the same process and represents, in the main, the product of mental recreation pertinent to a mind made clear and strong by outdoor life and exercise.

It was thus that the idea of organization with which to meet the expansion of his practice came to Mr. Sells. Projecting his imagination into the future he saw a large, complicated, and wide-spread demand for the services of accountants. To meet this demand would be needed increased personnel, a large number of widely scattered offices, a professional service not only high in quality, but uniform in character, a scheme of combining men and methods to produce results guided by general standards but governed by judgment.

The result has been an accountancy firm rendering a professional service but organized more like a corporation along lines of functional activities. Each office which serves the public in direct contact is designated as a practice office. Each unit so constituted comprehends provisions for personnel, technical procedure, management, and professional training, and recognizes the functions incident thereto. The practice offices are related to an executive division made up of departments which correspond to the functions of practice. A managing partner presides over the executive division and is collaterally advised by two other senior partners, the three constituting a council for the consideration of important matters of policy.

The success of the organization has been due in a large measure to the vision which foresaw the requirements of the future and made provision for meeting them, and yet Mr. Sells would disclaim any credit for having been a prophet. The practice today involves gross fees of several million dollars. There are 33 practice offices covering all the principal points in the United States, and, in addition, offices in London, Paris, Shanghai, and Havana. The staff at times runs to seven or eight hundred. The firm serves some of the greatest industrial, financial, commercial, railroad, utility, and insurance enterprises not only in the United States, but throughout the world.

It has been my privilege, with the assistance of

Professor Giles L. Courtney, of New York University, to write the editorial notes in this volume. From an intimate association with Mr. Sells extending back over a considerable number of years, I have gleaned most of the side-lights which have been thrown upon the themes. I have seen Mr. Sells in situations of all kinds but always with the same poise. In my experience with him he was always broad-minded, tolerant, generous, and just. The highest tribute which I know to pay him is to say that as I journeyed with him through trials and triumphs, my admiration became greater as I was privileged to know him better. In this case familiarity bred increasing respect. March 19, 1924, is a date filled with sorrowing recollections.

JOHN R. WILDMAN

New York, March 31, 1924

## CONTENTS

# I

# THE NATURAL BUSINESS YEAR FOR INVENTORIES AND FISCAL CLOSINGS

# I

# THE NATURAL BUSINESS YEAR FOR INVENTORIES AND FISCAL CLOSINGS

Definition. Advantages: low inventory; employees less employed with other duties; economy in time and cost. Suggested year endings for representative industries. Compliance with federal and state tax laws. Resulting benefit to accounting profession.

EDITORIAL NOTE: Habit and custom are largely responsible for present methods. Results of research conducted to determine natural business year in selected industries. Variation in application of conclusions. Other suggestions.

IN business, as in every other phase of human activity, we are prone to run in the ruts of custom and habit, to follow blindly in the routine of tradition, accepting it as a finality without questioning whether it is wise or best. For generations the custom of a large part of the business world has been to take annual inventories at the end of the calendar year without seeming to have any realization of the fitness of the time to their individual line of business.

There is really but one proper time for taking the annual inventory and closing the fiscal year and that date is on the completion of the "natural business year." By natural is meant the time when the bulk of the annual business is passed, when the busy season has given its best, when the harvest time of the greatest sales activity is over.

At the close of the natural business year we reach a point like a turn in the road, when we wish to review what we have done, to see the last 12 months in perspective, to find out where we stand financially. It is a time for new planning for the future, adjusting ourselves anew to conditions, seeing the most advantageous steps to take in preparation for renewed effort. It is the inventory, taken at this time, that will reveal to us the results of past effort and bring new wisdom to help us in building a better and finer future.

In this period following our year's harvest and in the lull preceding new seeding and planting, in our special line of business, for the next harvest, we have time to take an inventory. Then we are freer from the pressure of insistent effort, and immune from many distractions. Stocks of merchandise, too, are then at their lowest, so that the physical and mental work of taking an inventory are reduced to a minimum. Employees, too, are then less employed and can cooperate more effectively.

From every standpoint it is at the close of the natural business year that inventories can be made most easily, economically, and effectively. This period varies in different lines of trade and industry, for the natural business year that would be best for one would be the very worst for some other. It must be determined by the individual proprietor, the firm, or the corporation in harmony with the limitations and demands of their specific business in connection with general trade conditions in their respective lines.

There are many practical reasons to support the contention that most of the mercantile business of the country with which the consumer is concerned could best take inventories and close the fiscal year in the midsummer months—July or August. Those having heavy summer trade, of which there are few, could best take inventories and close in the fall—October or November, while other dates would harmonize better with other lines—the manufacturers of articles of domestic consumption, such as clothing and footwear, in March or April, manufacturers of agricultural implements in October, coal mining operations in March, automobile and accessories manufacturers in June or July, and railways in February or March.

In many phases of the nation's business activities uniformity is greatly to be desired. The date of the fiscal year is not one of these phases. What should be standardized, however, is the *principle* itself, the principle that applies with equal force to all, that the fiscal year should correspond with the natural business year whatever that may be decided to be.

Some have thought it necessary to close the fiscal year on December 31, in order to harmonize it with federal or state requirements in the matter of reports for taxation, but, as will be shown, the Government recognizes and accepts any fiscal year that the individual, firm, or corporation selects, so long as certain simple requirements and formalities are complied with in respect to details of method.

The law and regulations of the Federal Government are found in Law Sections 212(b) and 226, and Regulation 45, Revised, Articles 25, 26, 431, and 626. The vital points therein contained and stripped of legal phrasing are as follows:

The taxable year may be either the calendar year or fiscal year, the latter meaning, as used by the Government, an accounting period of 12 months ending on the last day of any month but December. The fiscal year must be the regularly established term of accounting of the tax-payer, but can be changed to the calendar year or a different fiscal year on giving the Commissioner of Internal Revenue written notice in accordance with the prescribed restrictions as to time. This may entail a partial return in addition to the full term return after the first change, after which annual returns are made.

Conducting commercial or industrial activities in relation to the natural business year means conservation of time, money, and energy. At the present time, when wise and prudent administration is so essential to cut down unnecessary overhead charges to the lowest terms, this question is of vital import. We are facing today two factors of excessively high cost, labor and taxation, each near the seeming peak of expense while production and sales are depressed. Whatever tends to economy in these days of trying conditions and narrow margins of profit should be carefully watched and considered to help to bring general business back to normal.

A glance at the cost in any concern taking inventory at a time when stocks are large and the sacrifice of business, including enforced shut-downs and the time consumed by employees who could be utilized advantageously in the conduct of the going business, would make an appalling contrast with the cost of the inventory at a time when the stock is the lowest and frequently there are surplus employees who can be utilized for the work without encroaching upon the demands of the heavy going business. Besides, in most cases this would come at a time when the manufacturing concern shuts down for necessary repairs, new installations, and generally getting ready for taking care of the larger flow of business at the rush period. It would show a large sum saved, the aggregate of which for all businesses would amount to many millions annually and possibly run into billions of dollars.

The tendency of state tax legislation is to conform with that of the Federal Government. In cases where the states have not done this and still require returns at December 31, it would be far more economical to adopt the light period of business for inventory taking and fiscal year closings upon which the federal return is made, and then make a state return as of December 31, or some other date as need be to conform with the laws of the state, based upon the book or estimated value of inventories at that date. The same may be said respecting reports required by other Government and state departments.

In most of the well-regulated businesses continuous book inventories are carried along from month to month. This is part of what constitutes an efficient cost system and for those businesses that do not have such a system and depend entirely upon the taking of inventories to determine values and profits, it would be well to change their system of keeping accounts and introduce the more modern and efficient plan of charging the stock account with the purchases from time to time and crediting it with the withdrawals for manufacturing and sales at the price at which the charges were made against the stock accounts so that there would be a very close approximation from time to time of the inventory as well as profits or losses made in the business from month to month. This plan is calculated to insure accuracy at the end of each month (which is checked by actual count in most cases annually, in some cases oftener) but if not absolutely accurate it is near enough for the practical purpose of making a state return that may be required at some date other than that used for the Federal Government.

There is another important element in the consideration of the natural business year and that is the profession of public accountancy, the usefulness of which is constantly growing in recognition and appreciation by the business world. It may be said that all of the states of the Union have recognized the profession of certified public accountants by legislation that is practically uniform. The Federal Government and the states recognize the value of the profession by frequently employing its members. Public accountants are called upon not alone for the periodical audits and certification of accounts, but in helping to solve problems connected with annual reports and to bring their knowledge and experience to bear on questions of taxation.

Because of the almost universal practice of making fiscal closings at December 31, the profession of public accountancy is overwhelmed with work for a few months following that date and has a comparatively much lighter practice during the remainder of the year. If inventories and fiscal closings were made at the end of the natural business year, there would be distributed throughout the year from time to time a vast amount of auditing, tax work, and kindred things which the profession of public accountancy has to do so that its forces could be maintained more evenly throughout the year and be able to render service far more valuable to business.

The public accountant has opportunity to form judgment upon this subject. The firm of which I am a member filled something over 4,000 engagements during the past year. The accountants worked unreasonably long hours during the rush period in order to give the service at the time it was required. This is typical of public accountancy conditions generally.

Let us accept the "natural business year" as our fiscal year and in the aggregate many millions of dollars will be saved to the business of the nation in countless phases of efficiency and economy.

Editorial Note: "Habit is ten times nature," the Duke of Wellington is said to have exclaimed in discussing the forces that are constantly at work serving as a balance-wheel for civilization and keeping social and industrial groups properly adjusted. Habit may be beneficial, or it may be harmful. It is habit of a beneficial character that keeps the farmer at his plow, the sailor at sea, and the business man at his desk. Without such habit, accepted by generation after generation, the entire social structure might be in danger.

But it is pernicious habit that must be guarded against; that must be controlled and altered. When in the light of increased knowledge, we continue in the old channels of tradition, we cast aside the benefits and advantages of constructive thought and retain the shackles of antiquity. Habit, and habit without intelligent foundation, is chiefly responsible for the unwillingness manifested by many business men to establish a fiscal year that coincides with the natural business year.

In dealing with this subject, Mr. Sells explains pointedly and convincingly the advantages to be derived by accepting the natural business year as the basis for taking inventories and making fiscal closings. Additional comment on these advantages would seem superfluous. It might be of interest, however, to supplement the list of industries given and to consider the natural business year of each. The conclusions in some cases, of course, must be expressed with reservations because they may be inapplicable owing to peculiarities which exist in the particular organization, or to climatic conditions that would modify the application.

For example, a manufacturer, engaged in a line of business that normally employs jobbers, may decide to perform the jobbing function himself and distribute his products direct to retailers. He would be called upon in this instance to store or warehouse the products until they were required by retailers and consequently his stock variations might not be in agreement with those of other manufacturers who distribute solely to jobbers. Or, climatic conditions may enter as an influencing factor. The field of dairy products is representative of this type of business. Because the production of farm products is dependent in a large part on weather conditions, the natural business year will vary in accordance with the conditions in the different sections of the country.

In a research recently conducted, considerable information pertaining to this subject was assembled. Conclusions of a general character were drawn from the reports contained in technical and trade papers, Federal Reserve Bulletins, and Department of Commerce Surveys, and from reports of labor employment and freight-car loadings over a period of years. These conclusions relating to some of the more important types of business follow. For the purpose of being specific, a definite closing date is suggested in each instance.

*Agricultural implements*. The period of heavy production in this industry extends from February to August and the period of light production from October to December. At October 31, shipment of orders from the previous fall and winter has been completed and inventories are low awaiting the results of the current fall campaign and the preparation of the new production program. It appears, therefore, that November 1 to October 31 is the natural business year for businesses engaged in manufacturing such products.

*Automobiles, motorcycles, and bicycles.* A year ending October 31 seems most desirable. Heavy production continues from January to August, while comparatively light production extends from October through December. The number of employees engaged in this work increases from December to June and decreases from July to October. At October 31 production is naturally small, inventories are low as plans for the coming year are being developed.

*Boots and shoes.* The variations in the quantity of production and in the number of employees engaged, as shown in reports, indicate that the major operations lie in the period between September 1 and December 31, and the minor between May 1 and July 1. Annual exhibits are held late in May and early in June for the purpose of introducing new styles for the coming seasons. If the business year were to end June 30, inventories would be low, and the operating statement would reflect the results of business in the various models of the previous year.

*Building construction.* The peak requirements must be met in the period from April to November. The period from December to February is one of decreased activity. An appropriate ending for the business year would be December 31.

*Cement.* The greatest volume of business transacted by these companies is with the building trades, road contractors, and so forth, whose activities are confined to the open seasons of the year. The heaviest demands on the manufacturers' facilities occur from May to September, while the lightest occur from December to February. December 31 ends the natural business year.

*Coal.* The heaviest consumption of coal takes place during the months October to March. Activity at the mines is greatest from July to February and decreases during April and May. At April 30 inventories are low and the deliveries for the natural business year are completed.

*Construction of pavements, roads, tunnels, and so forth.* The same applies as in the case of building construction.

*Cotton.* Cotton is grown from April to August and it is ginned on a large-scale basis from September to December. The warehouse stocks are largest from November to March. At July 31 the sales of the previous crop are known and inventories are at a minimum.

*Department stores.* The maximum sales are made from October to January and the minimum from June to August. At June 30 inventories are small and with the slow months following a survey of the situation can be made to determine the requirements of the peak months to follow.

*Dairy products (butter, cheese, and milk to be canned).* In the northern section of the country, the feeding season for cows ends in March. Hence, March 31 marks the time at which stocks of feed are lowest. As the new production of dairy products begins with the opening of the grazing season, the flow from storage decreases and the inventories are low at about the same date, March 31. In connection with canned milk, the consumption is greatest during the period of decreased production of the natural commodity. As the volume of activity at plants declines when milk production begins anew, the inventories are reduced to a minimum. Hence, March 31 would also be a suitable closing date for milk canneries. This date may be changed because of varying climatic conditions.

*Electrical supplies.* Owing to the activity in the building trades and owing to the demands of public utility corporations and railroads that are repairing their old equipment and adding new, the period of increased consumption of electrical supplies extends from April to November. To meet these demands, manufacturers operate on a heavy scale from December to June. At October 31 their inventories are low preparatory to the beginning of operations for the following season.

*Flour and grist mills.* In general the growing of crops proceeds from April to September and the harvesting from August to November. The mills are busiest from September to December. At July 31 the crops of the previous year have been completely taken up and the crops of the present year are being harvested for later milling and warehousing.

*Furniture and fixtures.* The retail sales are largest from September to December and smallest from February to April. Manufacturers speed up production from August to November and slacken down from May to July. June 30 is a suitable closing date for such enterprises.

*Marble and stone work (quarries and stone cutters).* Peak production in this industry extends from March to November, while low production extends from December to February. December 31 marks the end of the natural business year.

*Men's clothing.* Style changes exert a determining influence on the production policies of manufacturers of men's clothing. January to April and July to October are usually the periods of increased activity. At June 30 the needs of the spring season have been met, inventories are low, and plans for the next production period are under way.

*Oil industry.* The heaviest consumption of oil takes place during the spring, summer, and autumn months. As stocks are lowest during February and March, inventories may be conveniently taken and the books closed at February 28.

*Public utility companies.* So far as the natural business year is concerned, electric and gas lighting and power companies, street railways, telephone, telegraph, and radio companies fall into the same general class. From the standpoint of inventories, September 30 appears to be an appropriate closing date.

*Rubber goods.* The type of product manufactured has a vital bearing on the trend of production. Manufacturers of automobile tires are most active during the period from May to October and least active during the period from November to February. For manufacturers of boots, shoes, and clothing requiring rubber, the lowest production is during June and July. December 31 is a suitable closing date for the former class of manufacturers and June 30 for the latter.

*Sawmills and planing mills.* Lumber is cut during the winter and sent to the mills in the spring. Receipts at such markets as St. Louis and Chicago and freight-car loadings indicate that the peak production occurs from May to October and low production from January to March. February 28 ends the natural business year.

*Shipbuilding.* Operations in this industry are slowed down during the winter season and are at a minimum during January and February. If December 31 were used as the closing date, the financial statements would reflect the results of completed contracts, and the inventory would be low awaiting a survey of requirements for new work to be started the following spring.

*Sugar.* Refineries operate under pressure from February to August and production is curtailed during the fall of the year. October 31 is a suitable closing date.

The conclusions indicated above with respect to the natural business year must be considered in a broad, general sense. It must be recognized that the lack of application of a conclusion to a particular organization may arise because of any one of a number of peculiar conditions that might exist either inside or outside that organization. In a final analysis the problem must be solved by the individual enterprise. The various factors that influence the determination of the natural business year must be taken into consideration and an appropriate closing date decided upon.

A ready index, in organizations which maintain a perpetual inventory, will be found in such records. If a tabulation showing the inventory balances by months for a term of four or five years is prepared, it will be possible to determine by years the more or less constant period of relatively low inventory. The tendency may not be absolute because a business depression might influence the trend temporarily, but a practical conclusion could be drawn from the information as a whole.

Even though monthly balances are not obtainable from accounting records, it is possible that the recollections of executives who have had years of experience in a particular business will be serviceable in establishing the closing date which could best be used. In any event, a little serious attention to the situation will undoubtedly suggest the best basis for arriving at a conclusion.

It is true that many business men already recognize the advantages in economy and convenience that would result from the adoption of a fiscal year that would harmonize with the natural business year.

# II

# YOU CAN'T JUDGE YOUR BUSINESS BY THE PAST THREE YEARS

# II

# YOU CAN'T JUDGE YOUR BUSINESS BY THE PAST THREE YEARS[1]

Reasons for failures in business. Application to specific cases. Need for audits. Heavy inventories and stock turnover. Defalcations and frauds.

EDITORIAL NOTE: Record of failures for years 1918 to 1923, inclusive. Reading and interpreting accounts. The significance of turnover.

IF I were asked at the present moment for the most serviceable warning to a business man, I would say: "Don't expect to stand on the record of your house for the past three years."

The extraordinary conditions of the past three years cannot continue to exist. Already some reaction has been felt, and this is going to continue for some time.

As accountants, we know that firm after firm has made vast amounts of money during the past three or four years without deserving success. Firms which produced inferior goods, firms which have had bad management, firms which, under anything like ordinary conditions, would have been dire failures, have made money despite these things, and have made it so easily that it is no wonder some of them are deceived into thinking it must be a result of their superior ability.

Nothing that I have to say in this article applies,

[1] From the *American Magazine*, March, 1921.

with any force, to those years. But it is going to apply from now on. The real tug of war for business is just beginning. Firms which have made money simply because there was such a demand for goods at high prices that they could not help making money are going to find out that it takes something more than being in business to make a post-war success. A good many of these firms will go under.

If this sounds pessimistic, let us consider the ordinary records of business. At least 75% of all concerns started, fail. I have verified this statement by calling on an authority in such matters. It is as nearly correct as is possible. Men who start out in business seem to know so little about it that it is a wonder even so large a proportion as 25% succeeds.

Among our clients are all kinds of companies, from very small concerns up to railways, cities, and even governments. Big companies fail in almost the same proportion as smaller ones; but their affairs are so complicated that it is difficult to use them to illustrate single points. Small businesses often turn for their success or failure upon a single point, because their affairs are simple.

One of our clients went into business—we will say the wholesale crockery business—with $30,000 of borrowed capital. This client was a good buyer and an excellent salesman. He knew his merchandise and the markets for it.

Six months after his start he came to us boasting of his prosperity. He had been taking out five or six hundred dollars a month for his personal expenses, had paid his employees promptly, and had paid off $15,000 of the $30,000 he had borrowed. In his estimation his business was an assured success.

We went over his books. He had paid off his notes regularly; but he had extended his credit in the purchase of merchandise. His accounts payable had never been footed up. Almost all of his current bills were unpaid. He had enough of them outstanding to eat up every dollar of the $15,000 he thought he had paid back on his capital. In reality, his business had not made a dollar.

When he was told that he was just about where he had started he refused to believe it. And when at last he did see that in those six months he had made nothing but his own salary, he almost collapsed. This is not at all an exaggerated case, nor is it an infrequent one. I have known hundreds of men, even thousands, who have run their businesses as this man did, figuring on the cash basis only.

A merchant who sells cotton goods will figure in December: "Well, I had $20,000 in the bank on January 1; I've got as good a balance now, and I've drawn $15,000 for personal expenses during the past year. The business is in good shape."

On his shelves we will find bales of goods which are worth $10,000 less than those the shelves held last January. The amounts due him from the various purchasers of his goods are $5,000 less than in January. In addition, his accounts payable total $2,000 more than in January. In reality, therefore, he is $17,000 poorer than he was in January, even though he has the same amount of cash on hand.

It seems incredible, when the facts are stated in plain English, that men should look at a part of their business and take it for the whole; but consider the history of the ordinary man who works himself up in the world.

A shoe manufacturer, for example, does not, as a rule, develop from the bookkeeping department. He begins by working at a bench; then he becomes in turn foreman, assistant superintendent, superintendent, and finally he goes into business for himself. This is the regular road that heads of manufacturing businesses have traveled. There are only occasional exceptions.

Now, where does such a man's chief interest lie? In the production of good shoes. As a second thought, he knows that the shoes have to be sold; and as a remote third thought, he knows that some system of accounting must keep him informed as to how the production and selling balance. He hires a bookkeeper, looks at the cash balance every month. Perhaps he looks at the trial balance of his books, but his main interest is in the cash balance. When men who run a business in this manner succeed—and they do sometimes—it is largely a matter of luck.

As I said before, 75% of businesses started, fail. At least 50% of these fail because of lack of capital.

A man gets a brilliant idea and he cannot wait to begin. He starts out on a shoe-string, and fails, as a matter of course.

According to our experience, any man who wants to start in business for himself needs:

1. To know the business
2. To know where he is to get his capital
3. To work with enthusiasm
4. To know how to read his accounts

On a liberal estimate, only 10% of all businesses employ public accountants; 90% flounder along somehow, except where some man of unusual intelligence is able to read his own business.

An auto salesman, who ran a shop selling several lines of autos and of auto accessories, found himself in difficulties. This man was a first-class salesman and a good engineer. But the bookkeeper to whom he entrusted his accounts got away with a good deal of money. The owner ruefully examined the books, but found that he had no idea of how much he had been mulcted. So he sent for our firm to go over his books.

After finding that, apart from the peculation, he was doing a good business, we suggested that he have a monthly audit and report made, so that it would be impossible for his bookkeeper to get away with funds a second time. He assented.

Like most men, this man had very little capital. He was financed in great part by the auto companies whose machines he sold. But he had never had a clear idea of his financial condition, and this, together with the fact that his bookkeeper had defaulted, caused his relationship with these companies to become strained. Yet he needed their backing. Before he had received many of our monthly reports, he was sending copies of them regularly to the companies that were, or had been, backing him. The results were prompt. Relations became more cordial, credit was extended, money advanced. The president of one of the companies wrote him a personal note congratulating him upon the method he used to keep informed as to exactly where he stood.

With this approval, and with the absense of worry, he gained confidence and went to work with greater vigor. The war helped along, so we cannot credit all of his big success to this one factor. But war or no war, that man was on the road to success just as soon as he began to know his business. Added to his real ability, it gave him the power to get capital, which was what he most needed.

Inability to read business is not confined to small concerns. A certain large manufacturer, making three classes of desks, called on us to go over his accounts. The factory was working on a well-defined basis. On desk number one, the salesmen were instructed to get all the orders they possibly could. On desk number two they were to take any orders that came along; on desk number three they were to take orders only when accompanied by an order for desk number one.

"You see," the owner explained, " we are coining

money on desk number one, making a fair amount on desk number two, and not a cent on desk number three."

He thought he was right. But we installed a cost system for him, and before we had finished with it he had sent out a hasty order to reverse instructions. Number three was made the leader, and number one was sent out only on an order which included number three as well. The owner was right about desk number two; but by some process things had become badly mixed as to costs on desks one and three.

Another manufacturer was making both power and hand vacuum cleaners. There was an excellent market for both, but the manufacturer complained that he could not make hand vacuums cheaply enough to sell them at a price that would meet competition.

When we went over the books we found that certain fixed charges, such as insurance on a part of the factory, depreciation, a part of the executives' salaries, and so forth, were being charged to the hand vacuum cleaners. This was correct; but the fact remained that the owner of the factory would have to pay these charges even if he did not manufacture a single hand cleaner. Shutting down that part of the factory would relieve him of neither insurance nor depreciation, and his executives could hardly be reduced enough to make a perceptible difference in charges. If these charges were taken off the hand vacuum cleaners, he could make a price that would meet competition. And if he could sell enough of the cleaners he could carry the charges, keep the lower price, and still make a profit.

When we convinced him of this he went to work on a drive to sell the hand cleaners. The market was good; he sold them, and made a good profit and a real one. There was no error in figures here; it was simply a matter of reading them to the biggest profit of the concern.

One of the biggest factors in the development of the public understanding of figures is the income tax. Several millions of people have been forced for the first time to consider themselves in figures. Most of them have accepted the tax conscientiously. They have worked out their own problems or called on public accountants for help. But every individual who pays a tax has a deep and vital interest in the amount of that tax. Perhaps he has had no idea of himself in figures before.

Not only do figures themselves tell tales, but their relation to other figures in other businesses tell tales which can be known only to men who have handled many of these accounts.

When an employer hires his help among strangers, he is not likely to make the mistake of overloading his pay-roll. But many firms are family affairs.

A certain manufacturing concern of long prosperity was thrown by the death of the founder into the hands of the second and third generation. The business was in good shape; there seemed no reason for the members of the family to seek jobs elsewhere. It was taken for granted that when John and Tom and Harry grew up there were places waiting for them in the plant. As a matter of course, the important positions, and a number of unimportant ones, were filled by sons, grandsons, nephews, nieces, and even odd cousins of the founder.

For a time, the business went on successfully. Outwardly it was as sound as ever. Orders continued to come in, because of the past history of the concern. Then slowly, but surely, it began to slide down-hill, and finally it wound up in the hands of a receiver. Probably none of the family realizes to this day just why it failed. But had one of them been able to read his business without the veil of family affection getting between him and his books he never would have consented to the high wages and inefficient service he tolerated in the family.

Very often I am asked how large a concern should be, or what volume of business it should do, before it calls in a public accountant. Any business big enough to keep books is big enough to need an accountant to go over them. The biggest job I have personally handled was when, with Mr. Haskins, we revised the accounting system of the United States Government under the Fifty-third Congress.

Auditing the books of a big concern usually means auditing the auditor. Most big concerns possess an auditor who is an accountant. He acts as a check on the treasurer and all subordinates who deal with money. But there is no one to act as a check on the auditor! For its own protection, the firm employs outside public accountants so that no possible mistake or peculation can remain undiscovered.

Among our clients is a certain large company which engages us to keep such a close watch on its financial affairs that no employee of the company, even the president himself, can take a bond or a coupon from the company vault without one of our representatives being present to see him do it.

One of the very small jobs a member of my firm was called on to undertake was that of installing a system of accounts for a small catering business. The man had begun by serving suppers and dinners, cooked wherever they were served, or carried from his own kitchen. He was always hard-up for cash. When he received an order, he had to go out and buy the food needed and engage assistants. He had to pay cash, as he had no credit, but he very seldom was paid cash.

In his desperate need for ready cash he had fallen into the hands of the loan sharks. By assigning to them the whole of his payment for the order he held, he could get them to advance about 50% of the money. A good part of the other 50% went to them as interest on the loan. He had been doing this in lieu of anything better, when someone told him that if he had a statement of his business to show to a bank, the bank would lend him money at a lower rate. He had no idea how to make out a statement, and so he sent for us to do this for him. There was little data to go on, but we installed a system of bookkeeping for him, and in a very short time he had a statement, which he took to a bank and borrowed money on, at 6% instead of nearly 50%.

Many firms are beginning to employ accountants as the Chinese employ their physicians, to keep them in a state of financial health. With some large firms accountants are invited to make examinations at their pleasure, others want such examinations at regular intervals. One of the important discoveries my firm has made—a discovery made at the same time by many others—is that a year is too long a time to let books and accounts run on unchecked and without close analysis. Business health demands more frequent examination of its accounts than an annual one. In the affairs of my own firm we make a practice of preparing monthly statements, so that for practical purposes our business is run on a 30-day basis. Any man who can run his business on a 30-day basis is going to have a much better chance of success than one who runs it on an annual basis, because he is better informed as to its needs and demands.

Primarily, an accountant is not employed to give advice, but sometimes he is asked to, and then it becomes a part of his business.

A merchant, carrying silks, once cordially observed to our representative who was working on his accounts: "Now, when you have completed the work, do sit down and tell me your observations on the business." The accounts were correct and with that the merchant was likely to be satisfied. But our representative said: "You are carrying too much stock. You are borrowing to carry stock, and it is costing you proportionately too much. Reduce your stock 10%. Your business will not suffer, and you will be in better financial condition."

The silk merchant was bewildered. He had carried a certain amount of stock without analyzing it in proportion to its carrying charges. On thinking it over he admitted that a reduction of 10% would not hurt business and he accepted the advice, to his profit. Frequently a business is injured by carrying stock much too large to be profitable.

Very often merchants do not know how often they turn over their stock in a year.

"Your turnover is twice a year," is a frequent report, when the turnover should be at least three times a year. Then it is up to the merchant to locate the reason, which may lie in extravagance in buying or a poor selling force, or a bad selection of goods. Sometimes the accountant can help by pointing out goods that are holding back the rate of turnover, and the merchant disposes of these at a bargain sale and begins again.

There seems to be a popular idea that the stopping of thievery is the accountant's chief function. As a matter of fact, only a small proportion of all firms in business have any peculation. People always express surprise when some trusted official goes wrong. They forget that it is only the man who is trusted who has the chance to go wrong. There doesn't seem to be any limit to the number of ways in which a man may steal, once he has determined to steal. On a large pay-roll a paymaster may keep the names of a number of people who do not exist, and collect for them every week for a long time before he is found out. The cashier may simply overadd the pay-roll, and pocket the difference.

One very large fraud was perpetrated on a bank which used adding machines. The accountant examining the bank went through the accounts twice before he discovered how the fraud had been accomplished. The books seemed all right, but finally the adding machine lists were gone over carefully. The figures on the slips were correct but the totals were not. The operator had used the "no print" key to put in a figure to his own advantage and the machine had added correctly but had omitted to list the figure used. At the time of this fraud adding machines were more of a novelty than they are now. Since then, examiners have made sure that the figures on the machines are all there, and are all what they should be.

Graft is one of the most difficult things for an accountant to locate. The steward of a club may be receiving 10% on all bills sent to the club. The retailer who sells to the club scatters this amount through various items on his bills, and refunds it to the steward. Unless one item is large enough to arouse suspicion such graft may go on undetected through a long period.

One quite elaborate system of stealing was devised

by a shipping clerk who worked in a builder's supply house. This clerk would receive an order which made him take from stock one dozen electric fixtures. He altered the number on the order to 18 and sent the 18 fixtures out by a drayman who acted as an accomplice, and who delivered the 6 extra fixtures to the shipping clerk's home. When the ticket came back to the firm the drayman had again altered the figures to read 12 instead of 18. It was some time before the discrepancy between the stockroom list and the shipping tickets was discovered.

One of the common kinds of peculation, for which accountants are always on the lookout, can be worked without an accomplice. A bookkeeper and cashier receives a check from a customer, a Mr. R—. The bookkeeper cashes the check, taking the money from the cash drawer. He fails to credit Mr. R—'s account. A second check comes in, this time from Mr. B—. The bookkeeper deposits that check, but splits it in recording it, crediting a part of the money to Mr. R—, and a part to Mr. B—. A third check, coming in from Mr. S—, is credited partly to Mr. R—, Mr. B—, and Mr. S—. The fourth check the bookkeeper may cash and begin again. This process is known as "kiting." Just how long a bookkeeper can do this, without an audit of the accounts, depends on how long the suspicions of the firm can be lulled. The practice would soon be detected by a skilled public accountant.

Frauds in banks often involve very complicated

schemes and sometimes amazingly simple ones. An inactive bank account, where no statement is required because the holder of the account is not drawing checks, may be manipulated by the simple process of taking funds from the bank and charging them to that account. A teller can do this with impunity as long as the bank does not send out a statement. But, when banks are sending monthly statements to all their depositors, this danger is lessened.

A bank clerk may take securities which a man has put up as collateral for a loan and speculate with them, replacing the amount in securities before the loan is repaid. As few men ever list their securities by number, and care little whether they get back the same securities they deposited, so long as the value is the same, this kind of thing may go on until the bank clerk fails in his speculation and cannot replace the securities. Then he is likely to replace them by other securities of the same kind deposited by another bank client. Often, at the end of a series of such peculations, the thief, as well as the bank, has no idea of the amounts taken.

One cashier in a department store had a novel method of peculation. The store gave a discount of 10% to religious and charitable associations, ministers, and so forth, when it was asked for. Many people did not know that this discount was given. The cashier found out that fact, and began to examine the people who came to pay bills. When, by their attire, by the address to which the goods were sent, or by any other means, she could definitely find out that the people paying were connected with some religious or charitable association, and that they did not know of the discount, she accepted the full amount from them, marked the bill down 10% and pocketed the discount. Finally, however, she was detected.

Peculation is more frequent where a man holds two or more positions in the same company, or with different concerns. When a person keeps the books and the cash, he can more easily cover up any fraud. If a man is treasurer of several associations, he can use the securities or cash of one to replace those of another for some time without raising suspicion.

But all kinds of stealing are accountable for so little, relatively, in the field of business that everyone tends to overemphasize their importance. The bigger detriment to business are the men who plunge in and then fail, lose their own time, their own money, and other people's money, because they cannot, or will not, look ahead. The failures of business retard business to a degree that no stealing ever has equaled or ever will come near equaling.

EDITORIAL NOTE: Prior to the appearance of this article in the *American Magazine* an announcement was made by a poster which was issued from the office of the editor. It read:

HOW DOES BUSINESS LOOK TO YOU?

What do you expect of the next three years? Do you feel about the future as does Elijah W. Sells? Mr. Sells, of Haskins & Sells, Certified Public Accountants, says, "You cannot judge your business by the past three years." Since 1917, Government contracts and post-bellum extravagance have thrown an aura of golden prosperity across our business horizon. "But times have changed," says Mr. Sells. "It's what you do during the next three years that will determine your business existence."

Here's a lot of sound business advice that's abreast of the times. And from a man who probably has seen more failures from the inside than any other human being. It's an article that every business man—yes, every business woman, too—should read, and read carefully.

Many did read, and perhaps were mildly interested. Others read and perhaps took the caution seriously. Unfortunately, however, only too few who needed the information most were able to benefit from it as is evidenced by the high mortality in business reflected in the reports of failures. In the annual publication of the United States Bureau of Foreign and Domestic Commerce appears a recapitulation of figures compiled from *Dun's Review* as follows:

| Year | Number of Failures | Number of Business Concerns | Percentage of Failures |
|---|---|---|---|
| 1918 | 9,982 | 1,708,061 | .58 |
| 1919 | 6,451 | 1,710,909 | .38 |
| 1920 | 8,881 | 1,821,409 | .49 |
| 1921 | 19,652 | 1,927,304 | 1.02 |
| 1922 | 23,676 | 1,979,389 | 1.19 |
| 1923 | 18,718 | 1,996,004 | .94 |

The increase in the number of failures during the last three years over the number during the first three years is astounding, but at the same time it represents a not wholly unexpected condition to one having the foresight of Mr. Sells. The reasons for the increase in failures cannot be definitely classified, although if such a division could be made it is probable that the majority of concerns failed because of one or more of the causes enumerated in the article, namely, lack of knowledge of the particular business, inability to secure necessary additional working capital, lack of enthusiasm, and inability to read accounting statements.

The first three causes are more or less self-explanatory and in general are understood in varying degrees by business men. The fourth cause, that of an inability to read and interpret accounts, is understood only vaguely by a majority of those engaged in business pursuits. This situation, in a large part, exists because of the indifference which many manifest in the accounting requirements of their business. Until business men understand the value of the information contained in their accounting records, and until they so equip themselves, by studying and by giving increased attention to the subject, that they will be in a position to utilize this information, the condition will not be greatly altered.

The intelligent and progressive business man of today is not content to lay aside his financial statements after they have served the purpose of government tax calculations. He is interested in the figures as they may be serviceable in the revision of his manufacturing and marketing policies. He considers the accounts on a relative basis, comparing the amounts of one period with those of another. He tries to discover the operating costs that may be decreased through an improvement in his methods, and he is constantly on the alert to ascertain the effects of his expenditures as they relate to the volume of business he is transacting.

Another matter of increasing importance during recent years is that of turnover. Many manufacturers, wholesalers, jobbers, and other dealers handling merchandise in large quantities generally recognize the fact that the efficiency with which they use their capital is measured by the number of times that the capital can be invested and reinvested in their business over the course of a year. The greater the turnover, the greater will be the net return on the investment. There are, of course, limitations imposed in the determination of the average stock to be carried, brought about by the nature of the particular business, the practical requirements from a marketing standpoint, and so forth, but these factors may be given due consideration in the formulation of a suitable policy.

The smaller merchants, notably those doing a retail business, are still grappling with the problem. In a pamphlet issued by the Domestic Distribution Department of the Chamber of Commerce of the United States, the attention of retailers is directed to the significance of merchandise turnover and to the advantages of exercising adequate stock control. It is pointed out that although the importance of turnover is recognized and accepted, there are frequent violations of its most fundamental principle, that of overbuying, even among comparatively progressive merchants. An addition to the cash discount or an attractive price concession sometimes will induce the purchase of considerably more goods than can be sold within a reasonable turnover period. This entails the likelihood that a season will pass leaving costly merchandise in stock and causing, finally, mark-downs and sacrifice sales.

It is true, of course, that a merchant may be too conservative and buy less than could actually be sold. This is not, however, a really serious condition except when carried to the extreme, because, unless transportation facilities are very poor or the distance from supplies very great, a shortage usually can be adjusted in a few days, and often in a few hours. By providing himself with appropriate stock records and by considering the specific needs of his particular business, the retailer can avoid the danger of underbuying and overbuying, and can determine the exact policy that he should follow in order to secure the maximum turnover.

# III

# CERTIFIED PUBLIC ACCOUNTANCY AS A PROFESSION

# III

# CERTIFIED PUBLIC ACCOUNTANCY AS A PROFESSION[1]

The work of the public accountant differentiated from that of the private accountant. New York State Society of Certified Public Accountants. The Association of American Railway Accounting Officers. Advancement of the profession. The independent periodical audit as a safeguard for the public.

EDITORIAL NOTE: Proposed accountancy legislation in New York State. Resolution of New York State Society of Certified Public Accountants. Eliminating unqualified public accountants. Efforts of Mr. Sells in promoting accountancy to a professional position.

A PUBLIC accountant is one who is skilled in the science of accounts and who offers his services to the public for various purposes, such as auditing, which embraces the verification of balance-sheet items and accounts of operations and in many cases includes a certificate to accompany the statements rendered; examining and reporting upon the affairs of those engaged in every field of activity for the most part for bankers and others interested in investments; devising and installing new systems of accounts; revising and improving existing systems, and consulting as to classification of expenditures, the character, form and order of information to be prepared from the records and presented.

[1] From the *Manufacturers Record,* September 16, 1915.

The public accountant, unlike the private accountant, takes the view-point of an impartial outsider, does his work accordingly, and presents the results of his investigation in the form and detail which his judgment may dictate, which may or may not be in accord with the proprietor's views. The private accountant has to do with the accounts of an individual or an organization, and is usually in a subordinate capacity rather than in an independent position.

As representative of a very high type of public accountants in this country may be named the New York State Society of Certified Public Accountants, composed of accountants who have received certificates as to qualification and authority to use the title "Certified Public Accountant" from the Regents of the University of the State of New York.

As representative of the very highest type of private accountants may be named the Association of American Railway Accounting Officers, which is probably the most efficient body of private accountants in the world, having succeeded in developing for a most complicated business a simple and practically uniform system of accounting.

Although there are evidences that professional accountants existed in Italy several hundred years ago, and that they have been in Scotland for over 100 years, the profession, as it is now understood, is largely a creation of the last 50 years. Hence it is of very recent origin as compared with the professions of law and medicine. In the former, which dates from the time of Moses, there have been recognized degrees for its practice as far back as 1149, but in this country there was no recognized legal organization, such as the American Bar Association, until 1878, and in the latter it is necessary only to mention such names as Hippocrates and Galen to convey the idea of its antiquity. In England the Royal College of Physicians was projected by the celebrated Dr. Linacre in the year 1518, and this may be considered the beginning of the movement in English-speaking nations for disseminating medical knowledge through such institutions. Surgeons in England, however, were classed with barbers until 1745, from which time on a distinction between them was made and a distinguished branch of the medical profession given somewhat tardy recognition.

So far as the English-speaking nations are concerned, the Scottish appears to be the first to produce the professional accountant. The Edinburgh directory of 1773 designates seven persons in that city as accountants, although the Society of Accountants in Edinburgh was not organized until February 4, 1853, and its Royal Warrant received until October 23, 1854.

A Scottish accountant, Charles Selkrig (1760-1837), on one occasion was awarded a fee of about £20,000, which must have been a record for his time, and would be considered large even in these days.

In the United States the Institute of Accountants was organized in New York in 1882, and the American

Association of Public Accountants was incorporated August 20, 1887, but accountancy as a profession in this country may be considered as beginning with the Act of the Legislature of the State of New York August 17, 1896. This act empowered the Regents of the University of the State of New York to pass upon the qualification of applicants and to grant certificates authorizing the use of the title "Certified Public Accountant." Since that time 39 other states have passed similar laws, the qualification requirements under which vary in some respects, but are practically the same. They are, ordinarily, that the applicant shall have had a high-school education or its equivalent, two or three years' experience in public accountants' offices, the necessary moral qualifications, and shall pass the prescribed examinations. There is no national law in this country relating to the profession, and, unlike the members of the legal and medical professions and some others, members of the accountancy profession are not exempt from jury service, nor do they enjoy the right of privileged communication; they are not required to obtain licenses after examination before beginning practice, and anyone can take up the practice of accountancy, no matter what his qualifications may be so long as he does not use the title "Certified Public Accountant," to which only duly authorized accountants are entitled.

In the last few years accountancy has found a place in college education, the United States being the first country to recognize the importance of establishing accountancy in college curricula. The School of Commerce, Accounts, and Finance installed by the New York University in 1900 was the first of its kind in the world. Beginning in a modest way in that year, the school has had a wonderful growth until for the school year 1914-1915 it carried 2,852 students on its rolls. New York University's lead has been followed by 18 other institutions in the United States, which have established separate schools for instruction in accountancy and kindred subjects, 16 of which carried 5,183 students on their rolls for the school year 1913-1914.

The advancement of the profession of accountancy is keeping pace with the commercial expansion and development in this country. Its importance is recognized by governments, states, municipalities, railroad companies, manufacturers and large undertakings of every description, as is indicated by the ever-increasing extent to which the services of the members are requisitioned, as well as by the number of corporations appending to their published annual reports the certificates of certified public accountants.

The independent periodical audit is a safeguard and a decided restraint upon the officers and employees of any business. By means of it investors in the securities of corporations are protected and trustees of educational and eleemosynary institutions are kept informed of financial conditions.

And perhaps more to the point than anything else: The purposes of the audit are to detect and set straight irregularities, whether intentional or otherwise. It gives to those interested in the accounts of the business examined the benefit of a broad experience as to the method of presenting the financial condition, which is of practical advantage, at a nominal expense.

In Great Britain public auditors are elected, according to legal requirements, by stockholders at the annual meetings of corporations. No doubt the business world in this country would be better served if we had a similar law instead of leaving the selection of accountants to officers of corporations or boards of directors.

Perhaps, on account of the rapidity of its growth, however, there is occasionally found a business man who fails to understand that the members of the profession of accountancy must not be placed in the attitude of competitively bidding for work. Who would think of asking two or more members of the legal profession or of the medical profession to submit bids?

Editorial Note: The increased attention which has been given since 1915 by legislative bodies to the status of public accountancy is of interest not only to the accountant but to the public as well. While no definite legislation placing a limitation on all of those engaged in practice has been consummated, the agitation which has arisen among accredited accountants has caused to be prepared drafts of proposed bills that may be presented as a means of protecting and conserving the interests and welfare of the public.

That our present C. P. A. legislation was passed for the

benefit of the public and not for that of the certified public accountant was held in the case of *Goldsmith* vs. *Jewish Press Publishing Company*, Misc. 789, 195 N.Y.S. 37, where Judge Lehman stated as follows:

> The legislature, not for the purpose of creating a monopoly or new property rights, but for the protection of the public, has enacted a statute providing that only persons proving their qualifications may represent themselves as certified public accountants.

In view of the fact that the state legislature is competent, in its exercise of police power, to enact a law prohibiting persons from practicing certain specified callings without first obtaining a license, it naturally follows that if the legislature now enacts a law reserving the right to practice as public accountants to those who are properly qualified, it acts fully within the scope of its authority. It has been held that as one means of protecting a community against the consequences of ignorance and incapacity, the state may exact in many enterprises a certain degree of skill and learning upon which the community may confidently rely. If these qualifications are proper to the calling or profession, and attainable by reasonable study or application, no objection to their validity could be raised.

The New York State Society of Certified Public Accountants has recognized its responsibility to the public in this respect. At the meeting of the Society held in February, 1924, the following resolution was adopted:

> *Resolved:* That it is the sense of this meeting that the society approves of a bill to be drawn to provide that the practice of public accountancy in the state of New York shall be restricted to certified public accountants as defined by the State Board of Regents; such bill to provide for the granting of certificates to those who have been in practice as public accountants for an agreed term of years

prior to the date of the passage of the bill, and under such further provisions as the Board of Regents may designate.

Even though the favorable effects of the passage of a bill as suggested above will not be immediately felt, the need for such a measure is obvious. The process of eliminating from the field persons who are not qualified should be gradual but certain in its operation. Owing to the fact that there are many accountants practicing who have not received their state credentials, it is evident that a satisfactory adjustment of the condition cannot be accomplished by a single stroke of the pen; it is desirable, and only just, that these accountants be given every reasonable opportunity to avail themselves of the right to continue in practice. When the elimination as provided for by proposed legislation is completed, and only those who can meet the requirements as established by the Board of Regents remain, the profession of accountancy as it appears in the eyes of the public will have a new dignity and will enjoy the added confidence of those who require its services.

The untiring efforts which Mr. Sells has put forth in the movement to secure adequate legislation for the betterment of the profession are well known to those with whom he has come in contact. His enthusiastic interest in this subject as reflected in his inaugural address on the occasion of being elected president of the American Association of Public Accountants in 1906, has continued unabated. For this interest and for the high ideals which he has inspired among his associates, the profession owes Mr. Sells an everlasting debt of gratitude.

# IV

# THE ACCOUNTING PROFESSION: ITS DEMANDS AND ITS FUTURE

IV

# THE ACCOUNTING PROFESSION: ITS DEMANDS AND ITS FUTURE [1]

A business career. Benefit of educational preparation. The profession of accountancy. Brief sketch of its growth. Major demands on the public accountant: auditing, making special examinations, devising and installing systems of accounts. Profession deals only with conditions, facts, and figures. Equipment of the accountant. Inconsistency of legislation with business policies.

Editorial Note: Recognition of business as a profession by colleges and universities. Extract from bulletin published by the Graduate School of Business Administration of Harvard University. Statistical information regarding the number of courses given in the various departments of business in the School of Commerce, Accounts, and Finance of New York University.

Time was when attention was focused on the professions of law, medicine, ministry, and pedagogy as alone worthy a young man's ambition, but today the one greatest interest of this country, business, calls him with no uncertain voice to a career co-equal in importance and quite as worthy of his consideration from the standpoint of the intelligence it demands and its usefulness in the progression of the world.

In my practice as a public accountant I have been brought in contact with men administering pretty much all classes of business, and also with those administering the affairs of government—federal, state,

[1] Delivered before the College of Business Administration of Boston University on the evening of Wednesday, September 29, 1915.

county, and municipal—educational and eleemosynary institutions, and with members of various professions, and from this experience I have no hesitation in saying that our men of business are the peers of any of them. They do not seem to have the faculty of expressing publicly their defense to the frequent unjust attacks upon them by the many would-be reformers whose only qualifications appear to be glib tongues or facile pens. And if it cannot be said that these business men are always wholly blameless in their methods, I do say that the men of the expansive type concern themselves more with the character and usefulness of their productions than with the financial or money-making end of business, and that they are possessed of certain ideals in practically equal degree with men in professional life, and in a much greater degree than those in public life. Moreover, I have found that men in charge of the administration of business are quick to discern and utilize the knowledge and ability of other men—a matter in which you are especially interested or will be when you conclude your work here.

As proof conclusive of the importance of business as a career it may be stated that the great educational institutions of this country are making signal strides in this particularly practical field by the adoption of accountancy and kindred courses which will redound to their credit—as they should—and which will be of enormous benefit to the country's business interests. These courses have created a most favorable impression on the minds of the men of business affairs, many of whom in the past, we must admit, perhaps reluctantly, have looked with some misgivings on university education for those whose subsequent activities were to be outside the professions.

In your College of Business Administration the greater part of the courses relate directly to subjects necessary to accountancy education. The other courses, while not entirely unrelated to accountancy, relate more particularly to business administration. As a matter of education, the two—accountancy and business administration—are more or less interrelated, but there is a clear distinction between them in the careers that will be open to you when you will have finished your scholastic work. Without minimizing the importance of business administration, I can say to those of you who have chosen public accountancy for your profession that there is a great and growing field before you, for it is estimated that only about 10% of the public accounting work in this country is now being done that should be done. So, going to the public trained and equipped to discharge the many functions of your profession, you will not lack opportunity.

For those who enjoy ancient history there is some solace and interest in this subject because the antiquity of accountancy is well authenticated. Baked clay tablets found in Assyria reveal the existence of private accountants in that country as long ago as 464 to 424 B. C. But it was not until the fourteenth century in Italy that double entry bookkeeping was regularly employed. There are indications of the existence of professional accountants as early as the year 831, and in 1581 there was formed in Venice an association of accountants which, in course of time, came to have more power and influence than our present-day associations. There were professional accountants in Scotland over 140 years ago, the Edinburgh directory of 1773 designating seven as accountants, though the Society of Accountants in Edinburgh was not organized until 1853 and received its Royal Warrant during the following year. The profession in England today is represented by several organizations, the principal of which are the Institute of Chartered Accountants with a membership of about 5,000, and the Society of Incorporated Accountants and Auditors with a membership of about 3,000.

There is much that might be said of other incidents in the more recent history of accountancy, notably the organization of the professional associations throughout the world during the last 50 years. The American Association of Public Accountants was incorporated nearly 30 years ago—August 20, 1887. It is the representative professional body in this country.

But accountancy as a profession in this country received its first legal recognition some years later from the Act of the Legislature of the State of New York, August 17, 1896, empowering the Regents of the University of the state to pass on the qualifications of applicants and to grant certificates authorizing the use of the title "Certified Public Accountant." Since that time similar enactments have followed in other states, until today there are only nine states that are without C. P. A. laws. Societies have been organized in practically all of the states having C. P. A. laws, and these societies are members of and form a part of the national organization—the American Association of Public Accountants. This association has for its purpose the elevation of the profession; the consolidation into a single professional interest of all the various component parts; making uniform so far as practicable state legislation affecting accountancy; spreading knowledge of the capacity and usefulness of the public accountant; and giving attention generally to the affairs of the profession. The association now has a membership of about 1,200. When the time is propitious it is well to join a state organization which will bring you in contact with this representative national body.

Only about 18 years ago a well-known public accountant, anticipating the development in this country of accountancy as a profession and, realizing the importance of education for the profession, approached the president of one of our largest universities—a man reputed to be progressive—with a proposal to establish in his university a course in accountancy. The proposal was ridiculed and called absurd because universities taught only the arts and sciences, and accountancy, the president of the university said, was only a branch of business which had no place among them.

But this is an age of advancement, and that university did not long defer its recognition of the importance of the subject. After some of the other universities had taken the lead it established courses which, like this university and some others, went further than the original proposal in that they embraced the study of some features of business outside the category of accountancy. It is well that these added features should be included, for business in this country overshadows all other interests. It is so big, so important, and so susceptible of further development and improvement, that the opportunity for the student of its administration is boundless.

The demands on the public accountant are various. In this country today the work in general terms embraces: Auditing, which has to do with the verification and proper statement of assets and liabilities and of the accounts of operations, and determining fiduciary integrity; special examinations and reports on the affairs of those engaged in every field of activity, for the most part for bankers and others interested in investments; devising and installing new systems of accounts and revising and improving existing systems; a miscellaneous class of work such as making statements of the accounts of executors and administrators and special data for cases to be litigated or arbitrated; organization of administrative and other branches of business; supervising inventories and appraisals; the preparation of reports and sometimes certificates relating to these undertakings; and numerous other incidental matters.

The profession in the discharge of its functions deals only with conditions, facts, and figures. It has no place for bias, perversions, fancies, or narrow and contracted view-points. It calls for breadth of vision, discretion, tact, and diplomacy. The continuance of the advancement of the profession which heretofore has been marked is necessary in order to keep pace with the demands upon it. Its importance is recognized by governments, states, municipalities, corporations—including railroads, public utilities, banks and trust companies, manufactories—firms, individuals, and undertakings of nearly every description, including educational, charitable, and ecclesiastical, as is indicated by the increasing extent to which the services of its members are requisitioned by all of these.

Let us glance at the financial return. It is estimated that, with the members of professional organizations, their staffs, and other practicing accountants, there are from 10,000 to 15,000 engaged in public accountancy in the United States. Based on the past five-year experience of my own firm, I find that the average annual return per accountant is about $4,000. Probably this would be a somewhat higher average than obtains for all public accountants, but assume the average to be $2,500, which is slightly more than 60% of our return. If there are 12,000 people engaged in public accountancy the annual return would be, say $30,000,000. This, bear in mind, covers only about 10% of the possible field of public accountancy. Carrying the calculation further: According to the income tax returns, there are about 400,000 corporations in the United States, and there are at least 600,000 firms, institutions, or individuals engaged in all classes of business and undertakings. If all these corporations, firms, institutions, and individuals required the services of public accountants annually—a somewhat chimerical supposition no doubt, although in nearly every instance their services, if available, could be utilized advantageously, and the experience of my firm as to the gross return from each engagement, again reduced by 40%, be used—the annual return would be something like $300,000,000, or 10 times the estimate of the present annual return.

These figures may seem alluring, but you must not be carried away with the prospects they hold out. Anything approaching such a high measure of practice can only be brought about through the development of an adequate and efficient profession.

As large as the field of public accountancy appears to be from these rather imposing figures, and however proficient you may be at the outset of your career, it is not to be expected that you will have immediately a clientele sufficiently large to engage your entire time and attention. This leads me to venture the suggestion, even if it appears rather bold, that there is open to you a new field as an incident to public accounting—that of public office. I believe there is urgent need for the services of men who, by reason of their training and knowledge, are particularly qualified for consideration of and action on public affairs in general, and public financial matters in particular. The time is past when we can afford to continue to have untrained men administering such public affairs as call for expert knowledge.

There are many public offices available to you which would not require all your time, and your incumbency would enable you to foster and protect the business of the country which it is assumed you are preparing yourselves to serve. Your capacity for judgment, your knowledge of efficiency and economy, your high ideals—which of necessity as public accountants will be your principal stock in trade—and your undoubted attitude of fairness towards business, equip you for the undertaking, and would present a refreshing contrast to the characteristics of the average office-holding and office-seeking politician. You perhaps will need some practice in speaking from the platform. This can be obtained without any loss of time in your work here by debating your accounting problems and especially those dealing with public affairs.

It is surprising to find how woefully lacking are many of our public officers in the rudiments of accounting. Through ignorance or otherwise they seem to confuse hopelessly the most simple accounting propositions, and to start endless controversies on matters as to which—when the facts are properly stated—there should be no difference of opinion. Numberless illustrations of such cases could be cited. Let me bring to your attention just two:

Recently the governor of the state of New York, in a special message to the legislature, stated that the financial situation of the state was very grave and that it would be necessary to provide through direct taxation the sum of, approximately, $19,000,000 to meet certain deficiencies. Both the ex-governor and his former counsel published statements to the effect that the tabulations of figures on which the governor based his conclusions of the necessity for such a tax were erroneous, and that correct tabulations would show not only that no such deficit as the governor claimed was imminent, but that there should be no deficit at all. Without entering into the merits of the question, it is evident that either the governor or the ex-governor was far astray on the simple matter of tabulating accounts, and that the conclusions of neither should have been accepted by the legislature without further investigation on its part. In investigations of this character or in the preparation of the data in the first place in such a manner as to avoid the necessity of investigation, the accountant as a member of deliberative and legislative bodies should prove to be of the greatest public importance and value.

The other example: Our income tax law dealing with the manner in which the net income of corporations, and so forth, shall be ascertained, reads:

> Such net income shall be ascertained by deducting from the gross amount of the income of such corporations received within the year all the ordinary and necessary expenses paid within the year in the maintenance and operation of its business, and so forth.

In other words, the income account should be prepared on the basis of cash receipts and disbursements notwithstanding the fact that a creature of the Government itself—the Interstate Commerce Commission—especially provides that the methods to be pursued by the railroads of the country in ascertaining their income shall not be on the basis of cash receipts and disbursements, but on the basis of income accrued and expenses incurred. And most of the larger businesses of the country so keep their accounts. Yet it does not appear that it occurred to any of our representatives in passing the bill, or to the President in signing it, that there was any inconsistency.

My point is that if a public accountant had had anything to do with the drafting of the bill, the inconsistency would have been apparent to him at once. Moreover, the whole bill would have been more logically arranged and would have been stated in language so clear as to render unnecessary the flood of rulings of the Commissioner of Internal Revenue, some of which appear to be entirely arbitrary.

However evil may have been the enactment creating the Interstate Commerce Commission and the subsequent enactments extending its activities and retarding railway development, which in turn has retarded agricultural development and hampered business generally, it is to the commission's credit that it has held many conferences with the representatives of the Association of American Railway Accounting Officers, the most notable body of private accountants in the world, respecting the form of accounts for railways and has many times heeded the association's recommendations.

The affairs of governments themselves, federal, state, and municipal, are increasing in variety and complexity, and their relations with other businesses through the somewhat socialistic tendencies of the times are multiplied many fold. The qualifications of the trained public accountant thus appeal with special force to the conservative business element of the communities they would offer to represent in public bodies.

No doubt a legal training is of importance in considering the bulk of legislative questions, still many of them involve matters of accounts to such an extent that in dealing with them the opinion of the public accountant would be of particular importance and you, with equal propriety with the young lawyer, could interest yourselves in public matters and make yourselves felt in the councils of the municipality, county, state, or government. I, for one, believe that your influence would be uniformly beneficial. While it is not likely that all of you intend to follow accountancy as a profession, to those of you who do I urge that this feature of your career be given consideration. I believe that the time you may devote to this kind of work will not be found to be unproductive for yourselves or the public, and that ultimately your standing and influence in the community as well as others of your profession will be broadened and benefited.

One of these days, among other things, there will be a movement for legislation calling for compulsory audits to be made by the profession of public accountants. Should you then have some affiliation with public office you would be of great value in restraining legislation until we have a profession sufficiently developed to respond to it. The Massachusetts Act of 1903, as amended in 1914, requires corporations with $100,000 capital or more to file reports in the office of the Secretary of the Commonwealth, which shall be accompanied by a written statement under oath by an auditor, needs further amendment in order to make the qualification of the auditor professional. It would be a lamentable catastrophe, however, if the profession as it is today were compelled by legislation to meet the requirement of auditing a considerable amount of business because of the lack of numbers in the profession to do the work justice. Legislation in this respect should be by degrees and keep pace with the advancement of the profession, and you will have an opportunity to influence it when it comes, as it certainly will, so see to it that such legislation. while conserving the public interest, shall be or mutual benefit to business on the one hand and to the profession on the other. In any event, see that injustice is done to neither.

EDITORIAL NOTE: The present prominence which business training has attained in educational institutions of university rank is at once both striking and interesting. While the facilities available for this type of instruction had increased tremendously in the successive years prior to 1915, even more noteworthy progress has been made subsequently. In fact, it was not until recently that some of the older and more conservative universities have added courses in commercial training to their curricula.

In a bulletin entitled "Business, a Profession," issued by Harvard University, in February, 1924, a clear and concise statement appears relative to the importance of commerce and industry in America, and also to the motive which prompted that university to establish, in 1908, a professional school of business. It reads in part:

> Approximately 90% of the American people are supported directly by mechanical and agricultural industry and by business; the remaining 10% are supported by general business indirectly.
>
> The growth of America has been largely a matter of the growth of American industry and business. It is industry and business which have made possible our schools and colleges and our standards of education. And it is to business and industry that we must look for the continued growth of our schools and colleges, the development of the sciences, improvement in our national standards of living, cultivation of the fine arts and all that makes for a keener appreciation of life.
>
> Business leadership, therefore, merits, first, the dignity and respect accorded the recognized professions and secondly, the advantages open to them in higher education and training. Business is not a new force in the world; it is only its present importance that is without precedent.
>
> Modern business, governed by economic forces and social obligations, is the foundation on which rests the sustenance of life and the enjoyment of it by the greatest number. Furthermore, a sound and widely spread public-spirited comprehension of the economic forces involved in the conversion of natural resources into consumers' benefits, is the answer to

many national and international troubles today. Without such comprehension and its practice the art of living can neither be furthered nor preserved.

Higher training in the professions not many years ago was gained by the apprenticeship system; students worked immediately under a single practitioner in law, medicine, or engineering and in that way were trained and taught. But the growth of population and its increased financial resources created a demand for more men of professional ability and higher quality than could be produced through the apprenticeship system. In response to this demand the Harvard Law and later the Medical and other graduate schools came into existence.

The same forces which brought about the passing of the apprenticeship system of training in the older professions are at work today in business. Up to within recent years the apprenticeship system has prevailed in training business men. But the growth, the size and complexity of business and the increased pressure upon its leaders has rendered the apprenticeship system neither profitable for business itself nor productive of the benefits possible by affording men a professional business training. To meet the needs of business and the nation for professionally trained business men the Harvard Graduate School of Business Administration was founded several years ago.

At the time of his address at the College of Business Administration of Boston University, Mr. Sells had already witnessed the rapidly growing recognition which many universities had accorded business training. His assistance, during the early years of the life of the School of Commerce, Accounts, and Finance of New York University played no small part in the development of its courses.

Statistical information regarding the number of students in attendance and the number of courses offered in the various departments of business in that school is of more than ordinary interest. At the beginning of the academic year 1923-1924, the names of 7,216 regularly matriculated students appeared on its rolls. A tabulation of the number of courses given in the different phases of business activity follows:

| Department | Number of Courses |
|---|---|
| Accounting | 21 |
| Advertising and Marketing | 27 |
| Banking and Finance | 28 |
| Economics | 20 |
| Economic Geography | 9 |
| English | 9 |
| Geology of Commerce and Industry | 4 |
| Insurance | 6 |
| Journalism | 22 |
| Law | 7 |
| Management | 23 |
| Public and Social Economy | 16 |
| Retailing | 9 |
| Trade and Transportation | 23 |

Although the majority of students are specializing in accounting, many of them either being in or intending to enter the field of public accounting, there is to be noted a constantly growing demand for intensive training in the other phases of business indicated above.

It may be said that Mr. Sells' active interest in the subject of higher technical education for business in general and accountancy in particular, and his assistance in connection with the early work of the School of Commerce, aided greatly in the laying of the foundation upon which the present impressive super-structure rests.

# V

# COST ACCOUNTING

# V

## COST ACCOUNTING[1]

Growing importance of cost accounting. Estimated costs versus actual costs. Reasons for detailed costs. Three classes of ledger accounts. Cost system should provide for three things: materials and supplies in their raw state, materials and supplies undergoing process of manufacture with the labor and expense incidental thereto, and finished stock.

EDITORIAL NOTE: Present importance of cost accounting. Service of the National Association of Cost Accountants. Uniform cost systems.

THE subject of cost accounting is receiving increasing attention from manufacturers. They are realizing more and more how essential a knowledge of true costs is to their success.

Not so many years ago the business man had presented to him by his bookkeeper at the end of his fiscal year a trial balance which showed only a part of his financial affairs. By comparing the surplus, which we assume was shown thereon, with the surplus at the beginning of the period, he was able to determine what his gain for the year had been. Not content with this, he demanded to know *how* the gain had been accomplished.

The statement of income and profit and loss, crude at first, was then prepared. From this statement, as developed, he was enabled to see more clearly what

[1] An address before the National Association of Agricultural Implement and Vehicle Manufacturers, at Chicago, November 29, 1909.

the source of his profits was; to see what his sales had been and the cost of such sales. If his profits were smaller than he anticipated he realized that either the price at which he had sold his goods was too low or their cost of production too high. In either case he must know what his true costs were. Obviously, before he could fix his selling price he must determine a cost on which to base it; before he could reduce his cost he must know where it was too high.

Up to this point this information had been obtained from the general books and estimates of costs, but the demand for special detailed information developed the need of special cost accounting systems. In response to this demand the cost system came into being.

To the business man engaged in manufacturing, the cost system has become invaluable. It furnishes him with information on which to base administrative judgment. It enables him to determine which lines of production are profitable and which are unprofitable; to push the sale of profitable lines and retard or discontinue the sales of unprofitable lines. The cost system enables the manufacturer to determine where his costs may be reduced either through the reduction of expenses or through an increase in the production. It also enables him to allocate leaks and stop unnecessary waste.

The time has gone by when the cost of materials and supplies used in manufacture is determined by deducting from the inventory at the beginning of the period, plus the receipts, the inventory on hand at the end of the period. How long would the business man continue to employ a cashier whose only means of determining the disbursements for a given period was the inventory method? Why should not money invested in materials and supplies have as many safeguards thrown around it as cash?

To develop his business to the highest degree of productive efficiency the manufacturer must be able to compare the work of his departments, his machines, and his operatives. He must be able to gage the efficiency of his managers and superintendents, bolster up the weak points in his organization, and harmonize the work of the different departments. The cost system makes all this possible. It groups items of expense around units of service, and items of cost around units of production.

As applied to the manufacture of implements and vehicles the cost system presents an interesting study. The problem before us is to find the cost of the product in its completed state ready for shipment. Let us take, for example, wagons. Whether they are shipped set up, or in parts, the problem is the same. We must group the items of cost around our unit of production —the wagon.

Differing in type, style, and finish, as they do, we are confronted, however, not with finding the cost of a given number of similar units, but with finding the cost of a given number of units all of which are different in their composition; and, further, the finding of the cost of the various parts of which the wagon is composed. The elements of cost are three—first, raw materials and supplies; second, labor; and third, overhead and general expense. Obviously, if we are to obtain true costs our system must be so devised that it will guide these elements into the parts making up our unit of production.

Broadly stated, the backbone of the system consists of three classes of ledger accounts subsidiary to and controlled by the general ledger, namely, the materials and supplies ledger, the cost ledger, and the finished stock ledger accounts. These ledgers, usually of the loose-leaf card type, are supplemented by numerous forms and reports, which collate and summarize the detailed information and serve, in many instances, as posting media for charges and credits. In some cases they furnish special information, statistical in its nature, based on the same figures, although differently arranged, as those found in the various ledgers.

The operation of the factory is controlled by a system of factory orders which are designated as plant orders and production orders. Plant orders are intended to cover the extension, operation, and maintenance of the plant. The production orders cover all articles manufactured and work performed for the trade. Production orders are further classified into standing orders, special orders, and repair orders. Standing orders are issued to cover the manufacture of small parts of stock, while special orders are issued to cover the manufacture of wagons and such wagon parts as are not covered by the standing orders. All orders for wagons or parts requiring special work should be accompanied by full specifications.

An account should be kept in the cost ledger with each standing, special production, or repair order, showing as charges the cost of material, labor, and indirect or overhead and general expense applicable thereto.

Accounts for standing and special production orders should be credited at cost as completed parts, or orders, are delivered to departments where such parts are used, or to stock.

The raw material records form an important part of the system. They must be sufficiently elaborate to permit of an extensive classification in stock ledgers of the lumber, iron, paint, and shop material and supplies, in each instance providing separate accounts for each kind and size of lumber or iron, each kind of paint, and each article of other material and supplies carried in stock.

In the case of lumber, for instance, receipts of lumber should be recorded daily in the lumber ledger accounts, entries being made from the inspectors' tally sheets as to quantities, the prices being obtained from the invoices or credit sheets. The invoices should be charged on the general books to the "Raw Material-Lumber" account during the month in which the lumber is received so that the aggregate of all charges in the lumber ledger accounts for any given month will equal the total charges to the lumber account in the general books for that month.

Materials and supplies should be withdrawn from stock only on properly approved requisitions. After being filled, requisitions should be delivered daily to the cost department, where they should be priced, extended, credited to the proper lumber accounts, and charged to the appropriate production order or foremen's stock accounts. Before this charge is made, however, a percentage should be added to the green cost of the lumber for the lumber-carrying and kiln charges. These charges consist of the expense incurred on account of the lumber prior to and during the time necessary for proper seasoning and preparation, such as handling in the yards, insurance, taxes, interest, and other things.

To determine and control the correctness of the charges to productive work for such expenses an account should be opened in the general books called "Lumber Carrying Charges," to which should be charged the accrued amount of such expenses at the time of inventory and all subsequent carrying and kiln charges.

The requisitions should, of course, be summarized at the end of the month, and a journal entry prepared for the general books to give effect to the foregoing operations.

The remarks relative to lumber apply with equal force to the other items of raw material, such as iron, paint, and shop supplies, except, of course, in certain technical particulars where the material differs physically.

Labor, it will be remembered, is also an important element in cost. All direct labor in the factory should be charged to a plant or production order. This is accomplished by a system of daily time reports, properly approved and summarized by departments, posted to the pay-roll records, and distributed to the various orders.

The time of employees who are continuously engaged on the same class of work, such as engineers, firemen, truckers, handlers, elevator men, stockkeepers, and others, constitutes the indirect labor, in which instances time books should be substituted for the daily time reports. Such indirect labor will not permit of direct apportionment, and may be distributed on one of several arbitrary bases, the most equitable of which appears to be the direct labor hour.

These operations affecting the labor will be controlled by the general ledger through a distribution of the labor account to work in process, extensions and improvements, and other accounts.

Little discussion can be had on the subject of indirect or factory expense except as to the basis of distribution. Under the present-day departmental plan of organization, unit costs by departments constitute the prevailing method. Here the problem is twofold. Certain items of overhead or indirect expense must first be distributed over the various manufacturing departments. Having done this, the departmental overhead must be distributed over the work in process.

In the first instance, such items as heat, light, power, rent, taxes, insurance, and so on, must be distributed over the wheel, gear, box, blacksmith, and any other departments. The wheel department overhead must be distributed over the wheels undergoing manufacture during the period.

The question of bases is open to discussion—whether it should be one of cost or one of time. The time basis is the more generally used, and is founded on sound principles.

As was previously pointed out, our cost system must be laid out to provide for three things:

1. The materials and supplies in their raw state;
2. The materials and supplies undergoing the process of manufacture with the labor and expense incidental thereto; and
3. The finished stock.

As to the raw materials, we have discussed the ledger accounts dealing therewith.

With regard to the work in process, we have seen that the cost ledger provides a medium for recording the costs as they accumulate. As parts are finished they are transferred to the finished stock. As they are transferred, credits to the various accounts in the cost ledger are effected by means of clearance sheets, which show the quantities and costs of the parts cleared.

We should now look for a moment at the so-called "Finished Stock Ledger." This book contemplates an account with each part manufactured under stock carried for the trade and an account for each production order in the case of special orders. The accounts with stock carried for the trade should be arranged in accordance with the classes and sizes of parts. The accounts for special production orders should be arranged numerically according to the production order numbers. The charges to these accounts are received from the clearance sheets which record the transfer from the cost ledger when the parts are completed. The credits are obtained from the daily reports of stock shipped, which reports should be prepared on check sheets in the shipping department, one set of sheets for each shipping order. These reports should be priced at the cost of the articles shipped, as shown by the accounts in the "Finished Stock Ledger."

These principles in cost accounting may be applied practically to the production of any of the articles you are interested in. Such a system will give not only the actual cost of goods sold by invoices and in total, but the inventory of all articles of material and supplies, work in progress, and manufactured stock in quantities and values at the end of each month, without the necessity of shutting down the plant to make an actual inventory count.

Certain accounts can and should be tested by actual count of the articles shown therein from time to time without stopping the work of the plant.

The system will materially aid in the location of irregularities in the handling of material and supplies if they exist, and it will show the actual profits or losses of the whole business with such segregations as may be desired each month, or at such periods as the statements of operations are made. The system is simple, and yet efficient, and its operation, properly administered, will be economical. This must not be regarded, however, as more than a mere outline of some of the principal features of a modern cost system.

Editorial Note: The statement made in the opening paragraph of this discourse that "the subject of cost accounting is receiving increasing attention from manufacturers" was indeed a modest assertion. The development of industry in the United States and the profits accruing therefrom had been so favored by the conditions surrounding a new country and the liberal contribution of natural resources that for many decades correct cost data were relatively unnecessary. After many recurrences of panics and depressions, one of the outstanding of which was that of 1907, American business men began to realize the importance of a better knowledge concerning their costs. While the subject was receiving increased attention in 1909, the instances were somewhat sporadic, and there was little evidence of cooperative and general interest along cost lines.

Edward N. Hurley, chairman of the Federal Trade Commission, may probably be credited with having done more to awaken interest in this subject than any other one man. Following the establishment of the Federal Trade Commission, September 26, 1914, there appeared a series of pamphlets entitled, "Helpful Activities to Strengthen

American Business." The express purpose of this literature was: first, to extend constructive help to American business men in obtaining additional credits to which their business operations might entitle them; and, second, to aid in improving accounting practice and in establishing better cost accounting and standards of bookkeeping. In July, 1916, Mr. Hurley was widely quoted as having said that American manufacturers were to the extent of 90% without adequate and accurate information as to their costs. Practically two years had elapsed since the establishment of the Federal Trade Commission and there had been time for the collection of a considerable amount of information relative to business organizations throughout the country. Mr. Hurley was, therefore, not without fairly reliable figures on which to base his conclusions, and judging from his book, *The Awakening of Business,* what he did say originally probably was as follows:

"Intelligent cost accounting lies at the basis of efficient management.... At the present time it is estimated that 90% of the manufacturers of the United States are pricing their goods arbitrarily; either upon a basis which will get rid of the goods as soon as they have been manufactured, or upon the basis of what their competitors are charging."

Precisely what Mr. Hurley said originally is of less importance than to know that his remarks attracted unusual attention, and stimulated, with the supplementary urge of the tax laws, unprecedented interest in cost accounting and accounting generally.

Another instrumentality making for progress in the field of cost accounting has been the National Association of Cost Accountants. This association was organized in Buffalo on October 13, 1919. Mr. J. Lee Nicholson, a pioneer in the cost-finding field, was the first president and there were 98 charter members. The association now

(March, 1924) has about 3,300 members and 24 chapters, including one in Hawaii. The membership includes not only many in Canada, but some in Australia, the Samoan Islands, India, and Japan. The association is a cooperative service organization; it maintains a library, research, and question service departments, and issues semimonthly voluminous literature bearing on the subject of cost accounting. Incidentally, it is estimated by one of the association officials that there are from two to three hundred articles on cost accounting appearing monthly in the various publications throughout the country. The association emphasizes the bond between management and cost accounting, and stresses the idea that cost data are a means to an end rather than the end itself.

In taking stock of the progress which cost accounting has made in the past 14 years, it is interesting to observe that there are now about 100 uniform cost systems in use by various trades and lines of business activity, with about 50 systems in process of installation or under consideration. Not the least interesting fact is that included among those which have uniform systems is the National Association of Agricultural Implement and Vehicle Manufacturers, before a meeting of which Mr. Sells made the foregoing address on cost accounting, at Chicago, November 29, 1909.

The present tendency, while not ignoring any of the principles advanced in Mr. Sells' address, is towards what may be called budgeted operations and costs. This frequently takes into consideration future trends in the material and labor markets, including the items which enter into the overhead. The experience of many concerns during recent years with respect to inventories has probably had a marked influence on this tendency. Actual costs, obviously, may never be ignored, but profits will probably be substantially augmented by any system of cost pricing which takes into consideration market tendencies, even though the costs used for guiding the operations and figuring the original calculation of profits are theoretical. Regardless of how wedded one may be to a particular type of cost, it must be admitted that the purpose of business organization is profit, and that cost accounting may never become more than an agency contributing to the realization of maximum profits.

It might now be said that cost accounting is receiving attention which may only be measured in leaps and bounds.

# VI

# THE ACCOUNTANT OF 1917

# VI

## THE ACCOUNTANT OF 1917 [1]

Growth in membership of the American Association of Public Accountants. Legislation in various states affecting status of the accountant. Need for federal recognition and regulation. Extended use of accountants' services—prediction of 10 years hence.

Editorial Note: War problems emphasized the great variety of activities in which accountants' services are a modern necessity. Number of practicing accountants and state certificates issued. State legislation with respect to accountancy.

The American Association of Public Accountants, composed of the various state organizations, is today the representative body of public accountants in this country. Its membership 10 years ago numbered about 80. There were a few scattered practicing public accountants not members of the association, which would bring the total number up to about 100. The association now has a membership of about 700, and it is estimated that the practicing public accountants not members of this association will bring the total at this time up to about 1,000. If the same ratio of increase in the number of public accountants continues, there will be about 10,000 practicing 10 years hence. I believe that most of the increase in number in the profession in the future will come from your

[1] An address delivered at the annual dinner of the students of New York University School of Commerce, Accounts, and Finance, Hotel Astor, New York, February 2, 1907.

school and from other schools organized and conducting their work along lines similar to those of New York University School of Commerce, Accounts, and Finance.

The American Association of Public Accountants' Committee on Legislation is doing commendable work in its efforts to guide the state societies in their endeavors to secure legislation, but great difficulty is being experienced in the effort to obtain ample and uniform laws in the various states to provide for the admission of certified public accountants to practice and to regulate such practice. Laws have been enacted in New York, Pennsylvania, Illinois, Maryland, California, Washington, New Jersey, Michigan, and Rhode Island. These laws authorize the issuance of certificates, by educational and other boards, covering the designation of certified public accountant, and make it a misdemeanor for anyone not so authorized to use the initials or any other words or letters to indicate that the person using them is a certified public accountant.

Some of these laws, however, do not provide for reciprocity among states. Others provide for the issuance of certificates to certified public accountants of other states having equally high standards and where reciprocity is likewise provided for. In Pennsylvania the board of examiners has ruled that it has the power to give a certificate to an accountant in active practice in that state who holds a certificate from another state. The New York law makes no provision for reciprocity. It is misdemeanor for a certified public accountant of another state to style himself a certified public accountant and practice in this state.

There remain many states with no laws relating to public accountants and there is no prospect of obtaining such laws in most of them, as there are but few practicing public accountants located permanently in such states to look after legislation. The difficulties experienced in obtaining satisfactory state recognition and legislation will, it is hoped, disappear in the next 10 years.

The profession of accountancy needs federal recognition and regulation. The practice of public accountancy is to a very large extent interstate. All large firms of public accountants practice in most of the states; in some cases in other countries. These firms are organized with facilities for conducting their work in various states. You will find well-known firms having offices in from three to eight cities, including New York, Philadelphia, Boston, Baltimore, Pittsburgh, Cleveland, Chicago, St. Louis, St. Paul, Minneapolis, San Francisco, Los Angeles, and London. When a firm of accountants engages to make the audit of an industrial concern, with factories, warehouses, and sales agencies in many states, the facilities of the accountants' respective offices in different cities are utilized simultaneously on the work.

In the practice of the professions of law and medicine no such confusion exists, nor is the practice, generally speaking, of the same interstate character as that of the profession of accountancy. It appears, therefore, that it is reasonable for the accountant to hope for federal recognition and regulation. If public accountancy grows as the demand for auditing and publicity at this time suggests, it should be an accomplished fact within 10 years.

There is no legislation now requiring the services of public accountants. The recent banking act in New York provides that the board of directors of every bank and trust company, in the months of April and October, shall examine or cause a committee of at least three of its members to examine fully into the books, papers, and affairs of the bank or trust company of which they are directors, and particularly into the loans and discounts thereof, and that such directors shall have the power to employ such assistance in making such examination as they may deem necessary. The services of public accountants are now being utilized by some of the committees of directors of banks and trust companies in the state to assist them in making the examination.

In Massachusetts there is a law requiring corporations to file with one of the state departments a balance sheet and other statements duly certified to by an auditor appointed by the corporation for the purpose. There is no law, however, creating a public auditor and no state regulation of the profession of public accountancy, so that the auditors thus appointed are only such in name, not necessarily accountants qualified to pass upon the condition of the accounts. Some of the corporations, it is well known, often use someone manifestly not qualified—in some cases it is known that they have used the porter of their establishment—to serve as the auditor. The corporations so certified in many instances are subject to interstate regulations. It would be well if within 10 years the federal and state laws required auditing of all corporations and public institutions by qualified and duly regulated public accountants.

As the demand for accountants grows, so must the supply. It is a liberal estimate to make at this time that only about 10% of the work that should be done by public accountants is done. Where there are less than 100 railroads whose accounts have an independent audit, there are 900 more that should have. The percentage of banks that should be audited by public accountants to the number that are being audited is even greater. This is true of manufactories and other institutions, to say nothing of the commercial houses, and the wholesalers and retailers of various commodities. It may be confidently predicted that during the next 10 years the ratio of corporations and firms that are audited to those that are not will materially increase, whether laws are enacted requiring auditing or not.

The members of the Gridiron Club, at their dinner held in Washington recently, undertook to portray national conditions 10 years hence. Their projectoscope showed an emperor on a throne surrounded by his ministers. Education will be the public accountant's king 10 years hence, and, instead of ministers, will be surrounded by high ideals, good work, professional ethics and loyalty. There will be no jester; for 10 years hence the accountant will be, as at the present time, absorbed in serious problems.

EDITORIAL NOTE: Little did the speaker, on the occasion of the above address, realize the truth of his prediction that 1917 would have no jester, and that the accountant would be absorbed in serious problems. When grim death, stalking abroad on the battlefields of Europe, challenged the mettle of American manhood, no vocation gave more fully and freely of its members than accountancy. Many of the young men who listened to the prophecy on February 2, 1907, were among the number who volunteered for service.

The war with its problems did much to attract attention to capabilities of accountants and to emphasize the great variety of activities in which their services are a modern necessity. Income and profits taxes, an accompaniment of the war, called immediately for knowledge of accounting, and did perhaps as much as anything to require on the part of business concerns more thorough systems and accurate methods of recording financial data.

Indeed, it is to be noted that the year 1917 gave a great impetus to accountancy and did much to intrench it in a stronger position in this country than it had formerly occupied. Many of the war activities were responsible for this, as many matters not previously considered as requiring audit were brought into the group where independent judgment on their accuracy was demanded. While no statistics are available to show how the number of audited business concerns in 1917 compared with that of 1907, figures compiled in 1921 indicate that the number had doubled since 1907.

Again with regard to the number of public accountants practicing, no one was interested in or had the time, in the exciting days of the first year of the war, to check up on a question of this kind. But if there were 1,000 in 1907 it would probably not be an exaggeration to estimate that there are in the neighborhood of 15,000 now (1924).

It is a known fact that the various state boards throughout the country had issued, to October, 1923, 7,043 certificates, and that this, after taking into consideration revocations and duplication of individuals holding certificates of two or more states, represents a minority of the accountants who are practicing, particularly if there are included the many who are specializing in tax work. The laws of the states, except in two or three instances, do not prevent accountants from practicing. They do restrict the use of the designation *certified public accountant* to persons who have met certain requirements of the respective boards.

The speaker was less optimistic than coming events foreshadowed in 1907 with respect to state legislation providing for recognized accountancy practice. Every state in the country has enacted laws making this provision. The District of Columbia has recently (1923) completed the chain.

The accountant of today who looks back on 1907 has reason for much gratification at the strides the profession has taken. There is still much to be desired. But as time serves in so many ways to alleviate things unsatisfactory, so it may be confidently expected to bring gradual improvement to the conditions surrounding accountancy practice.

# VII

# WHAT SHALL BE DONE TO PUT EDUCATION FOR ACCOUNTANCY ON A PROFESSIONAL BASIS?—A SYMPOSIUM

## VII

# WHAT SHALL BE DONE TO PUT EDUCATION FOR ACCOUNTANCY ON A PROFESSIONAL BASIS?—A SYMPOSIUM[1]

Progress of the School of Commerce, Accounts, and Finance of New York University. Available field of accountants. Need for professional recognition of calling. Education as a factor in equipping the accountant for his work. Desirability for a definite outline of study for the student of professional accountancy.

EDITORIAL NOTE: Summary of opinions expressed in the articles of the other eight contributors to the symposium. Difficulty encountered by universities in assembling competent faculties for instruction in business subjects. Practice regarding the granting of degrees. Educational qualifications of members of accounting profession should be more rigid.

THE New York University School of Commerce, Accounts, and Finance has made marked strides in the interest of education for public accountancy. This school was organized in the fall of 1900 by my late friend and partner, Mr. Haskins, who served as the Dean from the date of organization until the time of his death three years ago. I believe the school opened with about 40 students. There are today over 500, the number having increased gradually from year to year. Dean Johnson and the members of the faculty of the New York University School of Commerce,

[1] An article which appeared in the January issue, 1907, of the *Journal of Accountancy*. It is one of a series of nine articles contributed by prominent educators and practitioners on the subject embraced in the above title.

Accounts, and Finance are to be congratulated upon what they have accomplished.

The American Association of Public Accountants is also to be commended for the active steps taken at its last annual meeting, in Columbus, for furthering professional education by authorizing the appointment of a committee on education.

I do not know of any statistics compiled to show the amount of public accountancy work performed as compared with the amount of work that is to be done in the unoccupied field. It is well known that only a small percentage of the railroad corporations in this country avail themselves of the services of public accountants in making independent audits. This is apparent from the published annual reports made by the railroads. It is assumed that the companies using public accountants to make independent audits append their certificates to the statements of accounts published. There is a growing tendency on the part of railroads to utilize the services of public accountants, but there is still a very large field in this direction unoccupied. I am informed that a year or so ago an inquiry was made of national banks in regard to the employment of public accountants, and the result of that inquiry indicated that even a smaller percentage of national banks availed themselves of the services of public accountants than in the case of railroads. There seems little reason for doubt that a very small percentage of manufactories, industrials, municipalities, and, indeed, all other classes of businesses and institutions, employ public accountants. Practically all of these concerns will, I believe, ultimately (either of their own motion, or in response to demands of the public, or by legislative enactment) require the services of public accountants.

We would all like to see the profession of public accountancy recognized in this country as it is in Great Britain and as are the older professions—law, theology, and medicine. There is a growing demand for the services of the professional accountant, as a means of responding to which the ranks of the profession must be filled with efficient members. There can be no doubt that the establishment of schools with high standards for preliminary training is the best means of accomplishing this end.

A profession is a calling or vocation based on a knowledge of a science that can be utilized and which qualifies one to serve in an advisory capacity in the conduct of affairs, public or private, the lines of which should be clearly defined. It is distinguished from mere skill. To attain a proficiency, and gain the confidence essential to professional employment, it must have back of it a distinct special training—one which will make available to the practitioner the experience and thought of those who have spent much time in the profession. The accumulated experience and thought which lie back of specialized instruction of this kind must take one of two forms—either it must be found in the practitioner himself, or it must be found in a professional literature. One or the other or both must be availed of by those best qualified to teach and systematically impart the science or knowledge to another desiring to qualify in a profession.

Skill is only incidental if not altogether apart from the educational requirements of a profession. One might be learned in his profession and not skilled in the practice. One might be a skilful instructor and not a skilful practitioner. A genius might acquire all of the educational knowledge required in a profession with much less application than another less gifted, but at the end of an educational period they would both have the same professional standing.

Let us not confuse the duties of the student of a profession and the educator with the practice of the profession, but let us see to it that the educational provision is made the highest that it can be, and, as far as possible, uniform throughout the country, leaving the quality of the practitioner for the public to judge after he has embarked on his practice.

Every student should be afforded an opportunity to acquire this elementary or preliminary training and to obtain a contact with actual practice after he has completed his educational course before he is permitted to hold himself out as competent to enter upon his professional career independently.

I would like to see a definite outline of study for the student of professional accountancy—one that can be made generally uniform throughout the country, in some such way as are the educational requirements of the other professions.

EDITORIAL NOTE: Even in 1907, the necessity for accountancy education of a professional character was generally recognized. The opinions expressed in the articles of the other eight contributors to the symposium parallel that expressed by Mr. Sells, and some of them are more specific with regard to the nature of the courses that should comprise this group.

In an editorial which appeared in the same issue of the *Journal,* a summary and discussion of the various contributions may be found. The following is an extract:

> We believe that every broad-minded accountant in the United States should take a vital, personal interest in the problem.... On the right solution of this question depend in large measure his own standing as a professional man and the value of his hard-won position as a public accountant. A high standard of admission and a proper professional training for accountancy go hand in hand; and both are essential to success in securing a permanent place for the calling in the little group of recognized professions.

After mentioning the fact that the views expressed are those of persons fairly scattered over the entire country, the editorial continues:

> Using another basis of classification, of the nine contributors five are practicing accountants and three are university professors.... The symposium, then, represents a wide range of territory and of interests.
>
> Considering this diversity, the unanimity of opinion on some points is significant. Every contributor, without exception, either in so many words or by inference, demands a higher standard of admission. Further, there seems to be general agreement on the proposition that this higher standard is to be secured, not by making the present C. P. A. examinations more difficult, but by widening their scope. The university men are especially strong on this point. Dean Kinley believes that the prospective accountant's course of study should cover more commercial law, general economics, private economic organization, money and banking, credit, exchange, public finance, taxa-

tion, and corporation management. Dr. Cleveland includes in his projected course of study almost all these subjects and considerable engineering in addition. Dr. Meade gives practically the same list of subjects as Dean Kinley. Dean Johnson says: "An expert knowledge of business as well as an expert knowledge of accounts is essential. Above all things he needs a thorough grounding in the science of business, that science which for two centuries has been called political economy." The university men, except Dr. Cleveland, are outsiders in a sense; but they are all in close touch with accounting work, and they represent the three universities which have done most for accountancy education. Their views are worth careful consideration. Among the accountants Mr. Chase and Mr. Sterrett emphatically endorse the movement for a broader education. Probably Mr. Sells, Mr. Miller, and Mr. Carlson, though they have not expressed themselves on this particular point, would take the same attitude.

It was in response to this demand for professional training in accountancy and in business that many universities throughout the nation established colleges and schools of commercial instruction. The scope and breadth of the courses offered in various institutions has been defined to a large extent by the type of training desired by the students and by the ability of university administrations to assemble suitable faculties. Because of the highly technical aspect of some of the advanced courses and because of the difficulty encountered in securing competent instructors, who usually find the business field more remunerative, the task of organizing an effective teaching staff and of presenting a well-rounded course of study has proved an arduous one.

Naturally enough, the colleges which offer the most extensive and intensive programs of study are those located in large cities. In such instances universities are in a position to obtain the cooperation and assistance of experienced business men and specialists who are willing to devote part of their time to educational effort. While these specialists frequently find it impossible to give their services during the business day, many of them are willing to sacrifice an evening or two each week in performing this worthy work. One may gain an idea of the number of courses given in the various departments of business training in a large institution by referring to the tabulation, which pertains to the School of Commerce, Accounts, and Finance of New York University, on page 66.

It is interesting to note that practically all universities and colleges offering instruction in business reward with degrees students who have completed a sufficient number of courses and attained a sufficiently high average of scholarship. Although this practice was not always followed in the past, especially when the instruction was restricted within narrow bounds, it is more or less generally accepted today. The degrees range from the Bachelor of Commercial Science, granted for undergraduate work, to the Master of Commercial Science for graduate work in strictly business courses, and to the Master of Business Administration degree which is granted to graduate students who have first received a degree in liberal arts or pure science and who later complete a required number of courses in business subjects.

In certain universities, students in the four-year undergraduate course are permitted to divide their work equally between academic and business training, receiving at the satisfactory completion thereof a Bachelor of Science degree. Thus far, the degree Doctor of Commercial Science is an honorary one and has been conferred only occasionally in previous years upon business men who have achieved especially noteworthy distinction in the field of commerce and industry.

From the evidence that we have today regarding the facilities for higher education in accountancy, it seems that the next step in elevating the profession must be taken by the state boards of accountancy and state societies of certified public accountants. The present educational requirement of a four-year high-school course which has been adopted by many states is scarcely adequate. If the profession of accountancy is to enjoy the prestige and respect which the older professions have acquired, serious consideration must be given to the educational qualifications of its members.

# VIII

# INAUGURAL ADDRESS

## VIII

# INAUGURAL ADDRESS[1]

Reciprocity of professional recognition among states. Need for a continued elevation of the standard of professional ethics; an increasing insistence upon the highest possible excellence of professional work; the encouragement and aid which many American educational institutions are giving in the development of accountancy education. Tendency toward standard prevailing in the profession in Great Britain.

EDITORIAL NOTE: Differences in the practice of accountancy in America and Great Britain. More emphasis placed upon details by English accountants. "His Stage Fright."

GENTLEMEN of the American Association of Public Accountants: I am deeply sensible of the honor and responsibility attached to the office of president of the American Association of Public Accountants. Although it originated in New York and although New York has a larger number of public accountants than any other state, at the time of the amalgamation last year of the American Association and the Federation of Accounting Societies, the number of public accountants comprised in the state societies outside of New York was more than three times the membership of the New York State Society.

The future growth of the profession, owing to the disproportion between New York and the rest of the country, depends not so much upon Manhattan Island

[1] Delivered at the annual meeting of the American Association of Public Accountants, Columbus, Ohio, on the occasion of his being elected president, October 24, 1906.

as upon increasing the numbers, the influence, and the reputation of accountancy throughout the United States.

I am in favor of the most complete reciprocity of professional recognition possible among the states. The practice of many of the public accountants in other states is extended to New York and the practice of New York accountants extends to other parts of the country. It is absolutely necessary, in my opinion, if accountancy is to grow as a national profession, that properly accredited certified public accountants of one state should be allowed to use that designation, under proper regulations as to registration, in every other state of the Union where there are equally high educational and professional standards.

I have from the beginning of the C. P. A. movement favored this complete reciprocity of recognition. It shall be my purpose during my term of office to advance this interest by every means in my power within the bounds of the constitution and by-laws of the American Association. Some of the states have already provided for this recognition and reciprocity, and practicing accountants are availing themselves of the opportunity to gain a definite standing in states other than those in which they have obtained their certificates. New York has not yet provided for this recognition, but it is my hope and expectation that within the near future this subject will have the earnest consideration of the New York State Society. I also hope that like consideration will be given in all states that do not have such a provision.

In proportion to the total number of certificates issued there are probably more accountants from other states practicing in New York than are to be found in any other state. These accountants include some of the ablest members of the profession. Their work in New York has been of the very highest order; they have won the confidence and respect of a large clientele in that state. They have been especially distinguished by their devotion to the profession, and they have rendered valuable service in promoting its interests. The New York certified public accountants should not, in my judgment, longer continue even technically to ignore this condition.

There are three subjects connected with the advancement of the profession to which I would especially invite your attention. These are, first, a continued elevation of the standard of professional ethics; second, an increasing insistence upon the highest possible excellence of professional work; and, third, the encouragement and aid which many American educational institutions are now giving our profession in the development of accountancy education. In two of these fields of professional advancement we have much to learn from Great Britain. As loyal Americans and as accurate observers we are convinced that America is far ahead of Great Britain in the character of our professional accounting work. In the field of accountancy ethics and accountancy education we are still behind our English brothers. It cannot have escaped your notice, however, that nearly all the changes and improvements in the regulations governing our profession in this country have been in the direction of a closer approximation to the standard prevailing in Great Britain.

I would particularly recommend to your earnest consideration the subject of accountancy education. The large universities and a number of private institutions have shown a most gratifying readiness to coöperate with the public accountants in training young men for the ranks of our profession. They are doing a useful and necessary work. It is our duty to assist them in every possible way, not only by our aid and influence, but by giving preference, wherever possible, in selecting our assistants, to young men who come from educational institutions. This educational interest could be greatly furthered if this organization would provide for a committee to consider the various questions affecting accountancy education and particularly the question of formulating a plan of accountancy education which, after being considered by this association, can be recommended to the different state boards of accounting examiners for their consideration, and through these bodies to the different educational institutions which now offer work in accountancy.

I thank you, gentlemen of the American Association, for the confidence with which you have honored me, and I pledge you my best efforts and the first claim upon my time for the performance of such services as the welfare of the American Association of Public Accountants may demand.

EDITORIAL NOTE: One receives from this address some of the breadth of vision enjoyed by the first president of the American Association of Public Accountants after its amalgamation with the Federation of Accounting Societies. In only one particular, apparently, might the views be criticized for anything approaching narrowness. Such point is where the author remarks that "as loyal Americans and as accurate observers we are convinced that America is far ahead of Great Britain in the character of our professional accounting work."

Lest anyone gain a wrong impression as to the significance of this statement consideration should be given to what probably was in the mind of the author and what he presumably intended the words to convey. The fact is fairly well established that American practice in accountancy differs from British procedure in certain ways. The essence of difference consists principally in the matter of routine. The American practitioner concerns himself with what he considers the matters of practical importance, often ignoring routine checking, which is more or less fundamental to British technique. Time devoted to consideration of principles often develops glaring errors involving large amounts. The same time devoted to mechanical verification might result in the discovery of differences covering only a few cents.

The superior value of the American theory and methods is admitted by some British accountants, even though the charge is sometimes made that American accountants are inclined to be superficial. One prominent chartered accountant, educated and trained in Scotland but having practiced in this country for many years, some time ago expressed to the editor a feeling of satisfaction at having come to America when he was fairly young in experience, and at having developed along American rather than British lines.

The development of American industry has necessitated unprecedented aggregations of capital funds. These funds probably could not have been gotten together except from large numbers of individuals through their association under the corporate form of organization. The employment of large aggregates of capital has naturally resulted in large volumes of transactions. There has been a large country with a large population to be served. It must therefore appear obvious that methods, to be efficient in the consideration of accounting and auditing problems, must be scaled in accordance with the size, volume, and importance of the matters involved. Moreover, it will probably not be denied that the procedure of British firms differs in America from that of the same firms in Great Britain.

With these thoughts in mind, it will probably be apparent that there was no intent on the part of the author to make an odious comparison. The compliments in succeeding sentences should be further evidence on this point if further evidence is needed.

Passing from the serious to the lighter side of affairs bearing on the inaugural address, there follows a newspaper article prepared by a professional writer to whom the newly elected president unguardedly confided how he really felt on this occasion. The article appeared in the *Chicago Daily News,* April 2, 1907, and was entitled "His Stage Fright."

It is lots more entertaining to hear Brewster tell the story himself than it is to tell it for him, for the simple reason that he can relate a story quite as well as he does numerous other things. Nor would it be so amusing if Brewster were not a man who has been everywhere, has seen almost everything, has done most things, and occupies a national position in the business world.

As a penalty for being elected president of an important body, Brewster was put down for a speech the next morning at 10 o'clock.

"When I read that notice," Brewster said, "I had a chill. You may not think that I'm a modest man, but it is even so. Since I was eight years old and flunked on 'The Boy Stood on the Burning Deck' at primary school I had never faced an audience, because I had intelligence enough to know that that was not my particular bent in life. To be frank, I was scared to death.

"They had kindly assigned to me a subject about which I knew nothing. I sat up all that night with a wagon-load of library books, trying to dash off a few brilliant thoughts about it. At 6 o'clock in the morning I sent down a hurry call for black coffee, and telephoned a university professor who was at my hotel. He seemed disgusted when he burst into my room five minutes later, with an overcoat over his pajamas, to find that it was not at least apoplexy or a bank failure; but he was a kind man and looked over my effusion.

"He said everything would be all right if only I'd remember when I got on the platform to pretend there was a man in the back of the hall to whom I was talking. Then he added, casually, that when I found my voice going—just gently fading away into nothingness—I was to stop and cough a little and begin again at the start of the sentence. He explained that never by any chance did an amateur speaker's voice leave him anywhere save in the middle of a remark. Also I was to take an easy attitude and not act stiff.

"My spirits had been low before he told me these things, but they ran out of my heels as I dragged myself to the torture chamber for that 10 o'clock meeting. I was pale but calm, with the calmness of despair.

"As they shoved me out on the stage I reminded myself that I had always paid my debts and that none of my ancestors was hanged for highway robbery. There were several million people banked in front of me, with six million more in the balconies, and they glared at me, but I looked for the man in the rear and began shouting at him.

"Suddenly I felt my voice going. I had no more control

over it than if it had not belonged to me. I turned icy cold with panic and then remembered. I stopped, coughed, pretended to study a word, and some man who belonged to the helping-hand society, thinking I could not see, turned a switch which let a huge cluster of electric lights right over my head blaze forth.

"My only thought was that I had been struck by lightning. I jumped 10 feet. When I landed, in my confusion I began at the beginning of my speech and read it all over again.

"A friend who had not been present at my brilliant debut put me down for a response to a toast at a big banquet later on. I reflected that nothing ever could be as terrible as that first time. Every one said that stage fright never attacked one twice and, anyhow, I didn't see why I couldn't do what other men did. This time I didn't call in my friend the professor. I dressed myself carefully and then nonchalantly departed for the banquet.

"When I found myself seated at the speakers' table next to the toastmaster, with a university chancellor opposite me, further down a senator renowned for his wit, a famous clergyman and a noted lawyer, and others as awesome flanking me, I turned cold again. In my pocket were my few impromptu remarks over which I had slaved. Each pulse beat sounded like a stroke of doom, and I awaited the fatal minute when I should stand on my feet with all the pleasant sensations of a man tied to a railroad track with an express train due.

"Somehow when my name was called I struggled to my feet. I had to hold to the table to keep from going right on up through the ceiling. I seemed to be swelling and filling all space. Moreover, in addition to these symptoms, which had been mine before, I seemed a victim of paralysis. I knew that I had my speech in my pocket, but I couldn't get it out.

"Suddenly I burst forth into words. I haven't the remotest idea what I said. I never asked and nobody was unkind enough to tell me. When I could slip away I did so.

"Then I let myself loose in a letter to my friend, the toastmaster. I said that if he did not want forever to separate me from home, family, friends, and associates for my being put in a murderer's cell, he would see that never again was I called on for a few trite remarks. I told him that I knew it was impolite to tell your host you had not enjoyed the dinner, but that I hadn't. The only thing I remember the taste of was the water, because I had consumed at least three quarts before I arose to my feet. I said it was all his fault, and he ought to be ashamed of himself, and I remained his truly.

"Then I took to my bed and the doctor said it was nerves and grip, but I knew it wasn't. It was just acute stage fright that hadn't worked out of my system. Anyhow it was painful.

"I would joyously shovel coal or pick oakum the rest of my life before I'd go through such an experience again."

# IX

# CERTIFIED QUARTERLY STATEMENTS ADVOCATED FOR CORPORATIONS

# IX

# CERTIFIED QUARTERLY STATEMENTS ADVOCATED FOR CORPORATIONS [1]

Records of loss through business failures in 1912. Duty of state to protect investors by requiring four reports each year. Distrust of administrative bodies in business. Quarterly report should show assets, liabilities, and operating results. Quarterly report idea gathering momentum.

EDITORIAL NOTE: Increased publicity to financial affairs. Quality of information put into reports. Business trends indicated. Corporation publicity would relieve the minds of the masses and the investing public. Desirability of a law making periodical statements compulsory.

THE official records for 1912—absolutely correct in dollars and cents—show that 13 railroad companies, having 3,762 miles of track, were placed in the hands of receivers. The total funded debt of these failures aggregated $106,964,497. The foreclosures in steam railroads represented 12 lines with 661 miles of trackage; a funded debt of $7,995,300, in addition to a stock indebtedness of $17,925,090, a combined total of $25,920,390.

This record, not including the liabilities of business failures, which amounted to $197,995,457 in 1912, summed up lost hopes to the extent of $207,378,887, a staggering situation for a year supposed to have been dotted with phenomenal progress. In certain quarters it is said that the records for 1913—now be-

[1] From *The American Banker*, New York, July 11, 1914.

ing compiled in several financial centers of the United States—will show even greater losses. The psychological depression of business which the chief executive of the country has uttered best expresses what the people may expect in the shape of a report for 1914.

The large industrial enterprises, sooner or later, will realize that the investor must be furnished with proof of the operating results before a funded debt can be created. Among the more progressive bodies a movement has been started to issue quarterly reports instead of yearly statements.

The certified public accountants generally are advocates of the quarterly report idea. The financiers of international repute are convinced of the practicability of the movement, and the bankers are now advocating complete publicity along these lines.

Unless the corporations adopt the system of four reports each year of their own volition, it should be the duty of the state wherein the corporation has been chartered to compel this system through legislative enactment, and this law should be especially passed for the benefit of the investing public. It is pleasing to say at this time that a few of the more progressive corporations have voluntarily adopted the system.

National banks, state banks, and trust companies are compelled to render statements to the Government and state officials at such times as the officials see fit to make their "calls," and this occurs about five times each year—and the date of the call is never known by the banks. Many of the important concerns which are great commercial bodies operating under state charters sit snugly back in their offices and await what is termed "the close of the fiscal year" and then report under their own seal, if necessary.

The general feeling among progressive officers of corporations is that the future success of new enterprises and the continued progress of less established corporations depend upon their ability to interest the investor. When the present great concerns were in their infancy the theory upon which a majority of them were conducted rested on the fact that the stockholder accepted his dividend and said nothing. If, perhaps, the holder of stock was not particularly impressed with the management he had the right to sell out. Of course, many corporations conducting their business along honest lines had due regard for their stockholders and used every method to please along conservative measurements.

During the past half-decade, however, a great wave of distrust has swept over the country, and at once the investor began to watch every danger signal that was unfurled. The muck-raker with his vitriol pen, the Wall Street writer with a grievance, the state investigations, scandalous magazine exploitation of the so-called trusts, and a thousand other factors have been the means to call a halt to the operations of the corporations that deemed it important to withhold facts and figures against the public. Instances have been given publicly showing gross carelessness in the management of certain chartered bodies; and the alleged proofs were furnished by writers of the muck-raking, showing stock that had been seasoned with water, pepper, and salt. But the writer of these stories —call them articles if you will—took special care not to mention the thousand corporations where careful stewardship resulted in an enormous business and which reflected credit to the nation.

The quarterly report, which should be compulsory, showing as it will the resources and liabilities, and the operating results, will do much to enlighten the public. It will bring about stable markets for negotiable securities. The quarterly statement should be issued by every public utility company, telegraph company, navigation corporation, municipal body, and every other interest having a stock or bonded indebtedness. It should be the province of the Government to demand this condition. The salient facts of a business enterprise of great proportions, and where the public is virtually part owner, has the right by moral law to demand an exhibition of earnings certified to by a competent and trustworthy certified public accountant.

Back in the days of the Phoenicians many good-sized corporations were in existence. Even during the reign of Pharaoh, Joseph created the first idea of the modern so-called trust. He cornered the food supply of Egypt to such an extent that the natives had sufficient for seven years. Thus, in the seven fat years, Joseph had the forethought to stock the storehouses for the lean years to come. The yearly report was admirably suited for digestion in those days. If the holder of corporate parchment failed to agree with the hieroglyphics printed thereon he promptly disappeared from the face of the earth. Perhaps the bond issue was wielded in such a manner that its force overwhelmed him. Then came the Roman period, and they, too, believed in the yearly report; so did the Dutch traders. The yearly report was issued every 365 days, because it was impossible to reach the public in better time. But today, with the wonders of modern invention and ingenuity at every hand, there is no excuse for so tardy a report as the annual one. This is a progressive age. We no longer can follow the tendencies that swayed the days of Rome. Even in those days the reports were more informative than those issued by some of our corporations of the present era.

Captains of industry in the days of long ago lacked the facilities of the present day, but they recognized and acknowledged the principle that shareholders who contributed money to make a venture successful were entitled to the speediest possible information as to the progress of the undertaking. Following this lead to its logical conclusion, it is obvious that the spirit of initiative and enterprise which prompted the early corporations was entirely in favor of the quarterly report if it were possible. But time would not be annihilated as it is today through modern invention.

The world is traveling twenty times faster than it

did three centuries ago. It is not too much for the shareholder to ask four times each year how his company is progressing. When this is done by the large corporations it will inspire trust and faith and will open avenues for greater business. The investor is entitled to a financial report. When a new stock issue is brought into the market the statement should be made in the official call for subscriptions that "This company, by a vote of its board of directors, will issue quarterly reports of its progress, showing facts and figures which will be certified to by a reputable public accountant." The quarterly report idea is gathering momentum; it is moving steadily ahead; its success is inevitable. A decade ago the originator of such a prophecy would have been considered mentally deranged. In 1924 it will be a source of wonder that the custom was not adopted 50 years ago.

In the march of present events the business world has no excuse for being six laps behind the 365-day cycle. My suggestion is open for argument, and who will deny the fact that the quarterly statement certified by certified public accountants of acknowledged ability leaves room for the entrance of deception of any kind? Honesty in business enterprise is an American desire—honesty to the investing public is demanded by the courts of law. The quarterly report can do more to create this state of affairs than all the mediation meetings that can be held. Whether a security is known as a first mortgage liability, or a trust lien, or a debenture bond, or any of the other hundred and one terms—the fact remains that it is an obligation of the company making it and nothing more. Now that the courts have granted the realty concerns the right to issue and sell bonds, although not chartered under the banking act, but chartered as a business organization—what is to prevent other business organizations from immediately offering securities of similar nature? But why should the investor be asked to place a single dollar without first having the certified statement from the expert who diagnoses the earning capacity, and so forth?

The publicity of the quarterly statement will mark a new epoch in American industries.

EDITORIAL NOTE: While it may be a matter of regret that the practice of issuing certified quarterly statements has not become as general as the author hoped and predicted, there is much for which to be thankful with respect to the increased publicity which corporations are now voluntarily giving to their financial affairs. One has only to read the daily papers to have evidence on this point. Obviously, financial news would be meager indeed were such information not furnished by the corporations.

It is still largely the practice for corporations to issue public reports annually. These are now generally supported by certificates of public accountants. Many such reports, particularly those of the largest and most important of the industrials, utilities, and railroads, leave little to be desired by the most curious stockholder. There has been much improvement in the quality of information put out by corporations. Notable in this respect is the tendency which has somewhat recently been noted not only to supply figures, but to interpret them. Such reports offer the best kind of evidence of a whole-hearted desire on the part of those who are responsible for corporate enterprise and management to acquaint stockholders with the true condition of affairs.

Notwithstanding the fact that the policy of corporations is still to issue formal reports annually, much interesting data bearing on operations is furnished to the press at shorter intervals. Some of this is issued quarterly; some, monthly. Observing the financial data which appear in the newspapers from day to day, one gets a fairly accurate picture not only with regard to the movements of individual corporations, but the data taken collectively, even without going beyond the mental processes, enable one to judge with a fair degree of accuracy the general trend of business, if not indeed to forecast somewhat the future. The impression as to the general improvement in business conditions as indicated by a mental accumulation of daily information when checked by a comparative tabulation of the net profits taken from a well-balanced representative list of industrials, recently proved to be correct. This comparison showed an increase in the net profits for the year 1922 over those of 1921 of 130%. The railroads, taken on the same basis, showed an improvement of only 10%. The conclusion to be drawn from these two sets of figures is that the railroads have not received their share of the general prosperity which the country has recently enjoyed. While there is, perhaps, no reason for holding a brief for the railroads, the purpose is to point out that without the increased publicity now being had with respect to financial affairs of corporations it would not be possible to develop impressions of this character from the daily press.

Mr. Sells, in discussing the subject of publicity for corporations, in 1911, in an interview with a reporter from the *Globe and Commercial Advertiser,* carried his suggestions to a point somewhat beyond that which has been reached, as follows:

"If the people were acquainted and made familiar with all the transactions of the government, there would obviously be need of less government, and, therefore, less government officials. This principle, applied particularly to the management of our industrial and manufacturing concerns, would obviate the necessity for explanations in regard to the administrative workings of the various companies now so insistently demanded upon every hand. For instance, if everyone knew who the outlaws of society were there would be an end to them, and the people would be able to protect themselves against such outlaws without the need of so large a police system.

"Corporation publicity would relieve the minds of the masses of the people and the investing public to such an extent that the demands upon corporations for explanations and defenses to suits would be very materially curtailed. Wide diffusion among the investing public of the salient things concerning a business corporation would operate to prevent the question in the mind of the public and also to prevent numerous actions at law. Management of corporations would thereby be simplified.

"We should have a law that requires corporations to file at some central state or federal point detailed monthly statements of operations, omitting, of course, those things that relate to trade secrets and secret processes. When this is done we will have a means of diffusing among the public information not now available under any other system. This plan would make plain to the people what our big industrial and manufacturing concerns are doing."

While the millenium in this respect has not yet been reached, it must be admitted, apparently, that marked improvement is evident. Much statistical data has been collected, tabulated, and diffused by the Federal Trade Commission, the Federal Reserve Bank, and the United States Chamber of Commerce. Collective information of this character would not be obtainable except it were furnished by corporate enterprises, and developments of recent years show a notable willingness of corporations not only to issue general financial statements, but to furnish many special reports and answers to questionnaires required by governmental bodies and requested by private agencies of various kinds. There is certainly cause for some measure of satisfaction as to the improvement along lines of corporate publicity.

# X

# PUBLICITY OF FINANCIAL AFFAIRS OF CORPORATIONS

# X

# PUBLICITY OF FINANCIAL AFFAIRS OF CORPORATIONS [1]

Should advertising expenditures be charged as an investment or as an expense? Historical sketch of advertising. Advertising has many characteristics of commodities of trade. Advertising which brings some new business or branch of business to the attention of the public may be considered an investment. Advertising which maintains a normal distribution should be provided for out of current operations. Publicity of financial affairs of corporations. Importance to investors and general public. Publicity should be given to elements which deal with capitalization and also to those which relate to earnings or sales. Unscrupulous attacks of politicians against corporations caused by lack of information. Need for systematic campaign that will organize this class of advertising.

Editorial Note: Interest of newspapers in address. Interest of advertising men. Quotation from address to Advertising Club of St. Louis. Press extracts.

Advertising is as old as man and dates back to that time when the serpent in Eden advertised successfully to our common ancestress the peculiar beauties and merits of his fruit. However interesting it might be to trace the development of advertising from that date through the period when the Greeks and Romans employed street criers to advertise losses and sales, and pictures on walls to advertise gladiatorial contests and other public spectacles, down to 1704 when the Boston *News Letter* was established, which paper contained the first known newspaper advertisement

[1] An address delivered before the Convention of Associated Advertising Clubs of America, Boston, August 2, 1911.

in America, and the rapid growth of this form of advertisement from the establishment in the first half of the nineteenth century of important newspapers in New York, Philadelphia, and Boston, down to the present time when the annual output of publications containing advertising matter attains the enormous sum of 35 hundreds of millions, for which it is estimated that hundreds of millions of dollars are paid, and to further trace the development of the profession of advertising from its inception as a science in 1840 by Palmer, of Philadelphia, down to the comprehensive advertising organizations of today, it would hardly be appropriate or necessary in a paper dealing with the problem of the position which cost of advertising should occupy in the financial statements of a present-day business.

It is not for a public accountant or indeed anyone to make the broad assertion on the one hand that advertising is always an asset to be carried in the balance sheet of a business concern as an investment, or, on the other hand, that it is always an expense to be taken care of through current operations. It is necessary to know the facts and conditions under which the advertising was done, and the relation which those facts and conditions bear to the capital employed or to be employed.

Advertising has many of the characteristics of ordinary commodities of trade; it may be bought and sold and has a certain definite value aside from that of the material and physical labor of which it is composed and, according to its application, as is the case with any other commodity, may, with propriety, be carried as an investment in the balance sheet of a going concern. It differs, however, from other commodities in that the benefits to be derived are limited to the advertiser, and cannot be dissociated from the particular thing or business advertised and as such disposed of to another, in which respect it is identical with good-will. And just as opinions and policies differ as to the extent to which good-will, patents, and kindred things should be regarded as an investment, they differ as to advertising. But if it can be shown that a going concern has something of real value in its good name and good-will, something that could be realized upon in any disposition of its business and upon which as an investment it is receiving satisfactory returns, there should be no objection to treating it as an investment and the same argument holds true of advertising which for the purpose of this illustration is a component of good-will.

A person, firm, or company, at the outset of an undertaking which has something to dispose of not previously known to the public, or for which superior merit may be claimed, should undertake to provide sufficient capital not only for plant and working materials but for advertising, in order to adequately bring to the attention of the public the merits of that which is to be disposed of. In such a case, the amount so provided and spent might with all propriety be considered as an investment and carried as such in the balance sheet, and in any disposition of the business would have a good-will value depending upon the returns of the business. On the other hand, an old and established business, such, for instance, as a mutual assurance association, would not be justified in, or have any reason for, carrying as an investment the expenditures which it might make for advertising, for, as such, it is not an asset which could be realized and distributed; it has no place as good-will value to the association whose business could not be sold; it is not a thing for which new capital could be raised, and so it would not be practical to consider it as an investment.

Generally speaking, such advertising as may be done for the purpose of bringing some new business, or branch of business, some new or improved article, or articles, to the attention of the public, which has a direct effect in creating or measurably increasing the good-will of a business undertaking, may be considered as an investment in that there has been an appreciable increase in the amount of capital employed; such advertising as may be done to maintain a normal distribution or to keep the name and nature of a business before the public or for the purpose of calling attention to special temporary prices of articles, while having some effect upon the good-will of the business, should not require further capital and should be provided for out of its current operations; in other words, should be considered as an expense.

Between the extremes, say of a newly started proprietary medicine business, the principal asset of which might be its advertising, and an old established mutual assurance association with no asset of that nature, would fall all the other undertakings which advertise, or depend in any degree upon publicity for the marketing of what they have to dispose of.

Given the purposes and conditions of the advertising and the general policy of the management of an undertaking in regard to such expenditures, its correct classification as an investment or an expense is not difficult to determine. But frequently it is difficult to ascertain the purpose, the conditions, and the policy upon which to determine the application, as between investment and expense, of the cost of advertising.

Recognizing, as any one must, who sees the daily papers and the current magazines and kindred publications, the strides that have been made in the science of advertising in latter years, and the success of advertising agents in putting their matter in such form and through such mediums as to reach the greatest number of their possible consumers, and recognizing also the infinite and increasing variety of the things which apparently it is advantageous to advertise, I venture to suggest a new field of advertising, with a firm conviction that it will arrest attention. It is, I believe, a field which has not been entered in a systematic and scientific manner—I mean the proper and adequate advertising of the financial affairs of the corporations in which the public is interested, either directly as shareholders or indirectly through their influence upon general business conditions.

However meritorious may be advertising of the character we are accustomed to, advertising the financial affairs of corporations is of far greater public importance, especially at this time when there is so much unjust agitation against corporate affairs; and advertising agents have a public duty in this connection that can and should be performed, the effects of which should be far reaching and of inestimable public benefit.

In my experience as a public accountant, I have had to do with the financial affairs not only of practically all kinds of corporations but with those of the Government, states, and municipalities, and have come in more or less intimate contact with many of the various officers and managers of all of them; and it is based upon this experience that I have formed my judgment that the managements of corporations are generally honest and, as compared with those of public affairs, more economical and efficient; that there is far more dishonesty among politicians and office holders than among corporation managers.

I also base upon this experience my opinion that full publicity of the affairs of corporations would be beneficial not only to the public but to the corporations themselves, as the actions and investigations brought about by the public uneasiness would be largely forestalled thereby. But to obtain these results, full publicity will be necessary and the public will have to be satisfied that the figures contained in the publications are accurate. Certificates of reputable public accountants to be made a part of such publications will undoubtedly have an influence in attaining this end. In order that an advertising man may intelligently canvass this class of business, he should be able not only to impress the managements with the desirability of such publicity, but he should have some knowledge of the form and the amount of detail which his public will require, and with anything *less* than which it will *not* be satisfied. That the affairs of a business organization are of no concern to anyone except those responsible for its creation and continuance is sound doctrine, and may be applied to small affairs without detriment; but in this country where corporations with large affairs have become the prey of politicians to such extent as seriously to retard progression because their financial affairs are not generally understood, these corporations are confronted with special conditions to meet or mitigate which they should forego certain of their rights of privacy, and I believe they would be willing to accept the counter-effect of publicity by making known to the public the condition of their affairs in such terms as cannot be misunderstood. This refers to corporations whose securities are quoted and dealt in and in whose affairs the public is concerned.

The proposition divides itself into two essential elements:

First: That dealing with capitalization which embraces all the fixed, liquid, floating, and current assets on the one hand and liabilities, both funded and current, on the other. In the preparation of this information, nothing should be hidden and all essential details given.

Second: That dealing with the operations which relate to earnings or sales. Beginning with the total amount of such earnings or sales fully classified, there should be shown successively the allowances thereon, the direct costs, consisting of labor, material, and incidental expenses, the general expenses, the fixed charges for taxes, interest, sinking funds, and finally the balance, if any available, and its application for extensions of the business, betterments, dividends, and so forth, and the remainder to be carried to the reserve, surplus, and profit and loss accounts.

These details need not, and indeed should not, disclose what are generally regarded as trade secrets—I mean by this, certain processes and trade affairs which from their nature should be kept secret and not disclosed to competitors and others.

There should be uniformity of publicity for businesses of a like character.

It is my opinion that the present-day inertia of business is due more to the unwarranted agitation of the politicians against corporations than to any other one cause. If the affairs of all corporations were generally made known, the voting masses would not be misled by the unscrupulous attacks of politicians, many of whom do not hesitate to use any and all means to attract votes.

The daily press, magazines, and kindred publications are the natural mediums through which the knowledge of corporate affairs should reach the public. The cost to the corporations of this publicity would be more than offset by the reduction in the expense of lobbying, defense against unjust legislation and blackmailing legislators; and moreover in some cases a part of the cost of such publicity could very properly be charged as an investment while the cost of lobbying, defense against unjust legislation, and meeting the demands of blackmailing legislators must without question *all* be charged to expense.

It could not be said that all corporations are free from censure, but publicity would act as a restraint upon these and would put in a fair light before the public those institutions which are entitled to the credit for the great commercial development of this country.

Many corporations issue printed annual reports, and some of them are published in the daily papers in abbreviated form. All corporations should issue full reports to their stockholders and should publish them generally for the enlightenment of the investing and voting public.

When a systematic campaign shall have been organized for this class of advertising, it will be the particular province of the advertising organizations to determine the character of the publications that these financial affairs should appear in, but I venture to suggest that if, in addition to reaching the investing public through the conservative press, they are also placed in the popular newspapers, and periodicals with the large circulations, they would be such plain contradictions of many of their articles attacking corporate affairs that they would have a salient influence in a fertile field, the voting public. With no matter what skill advertising matter is prepared and with no matter how much judgment it is placed to reach the public, the maximum of good results cannot be attained if the general business of the country is abnormally depressed, and the advertising agents, as much as anyone else, are vitally interested to see that the causes of these depressions are removed. And in removing or impairing the effect of one of the chief of them, the continual attacks on business corporations, the advertising agents stand in a position to perform a great public duty, by obtaining and giving scientific publicity to the affairs of these corporations.

If my opinion that full publicity of corporate affairs would show them generally in a meritorious light is not shared by all, at least all will agree that it would afford a means of obtaining a fairer public judgment of them, and if it did not free them altogether from the unscrupulous attacks, which seem to have no other purpose than that of pandering to the voting masses, publicity would go far toward counteracting them and it would furnish some relief to the unwarranted and unjust restriction upon the development of the resources of this country.

Editorial Note: This address attracted the attention of the press not only because it contained a practical suggestion looking towards better cooperation between the Government and the public on one hand, and the corporations on the other, but on account of the natural interest of newspaper publishing companies. Without attempting to fix accurately the time when the attitude of the Government towards corporations became acutely antagonistic, it is a well-known fact that the breach was still widening in 1911 when the address was delivered. The thoughts expressed by the author came, therefore, as a constructive suggestion, which was seized upon with avidity by the newspapers, if for no other reason than that it had strong news value.

Advertising men, of course, welcomed the suggestion with delight. They found in the address not only a thought with respect to a new source of income, but from the discussion with regard to capitalizing advertising expenditures, support from an unbiased source, in favor, under certain circumstances, of deferring and spreading advertising expense. The address was, therefore, given wide publicity by advertising men. It was reprinted and distributed freely by the Quoin Club, an organization comprised of representative men in the advertising field.

The substance of the address was used again by the author under the title of "Advertising as a Business Asset," in April, 1916, before the Advertising Club of Saint Louis. On this occasion Mr. Sells proved himself a worthy exponent of publicity by telling the assembled company, incidentally, something of the history of accountancy and of the capacity and usefulness of the public accountant.

"The demands of the public accountant," said Mr. Sells, "are various. The work in general embraces: auditing, which has to do with the verification and proper statement of assets and liabilities and the accounts of operations, and determination of fiduciary integrity; special examinations and reports on the affairs of those engaged in every field of activity, for the most part for bankers and others interested in investments; devising and installing new systems of accounts and revising and improving existing systems; a miscellaneous class of work such as making statements of the accounts of executors and administrators and special data for cases to be litigated or arbitrated; organization of administrative and other branches of business; supervising inventories and appraisals; preparation of reports and frequently certificates relating to these undertakings; and numerous other incidental matters."

There was at the time of the Saint Louis address much discussion over the inconsistency of the income tax law. The outstanding cause of criticism was the wording of the law which provided that corporations should make returns of net income based on income received and expenses paid within the taxable year regardless of income earned, whether or not received, and expenses incurred, whether or not paid. With his characteristic courage the author took advantage of the opportunity afforded him in appearing before the Advertising Club of Saint Louis to call attention to the inconsistency of the law as follows:

"Let me bring to your attention just one case, not wholly unrelated to our specific topic: Our income tax law dealing with the manner in which the net income of corporations, and so forth, shall be ascertained reads:

"Such net income shall be ascertained by deducting from the gross amount of the income of such corporations received within the year all the ordinary and necessary expenses paid within the year in the maintenance and operation of its business, and so forth.

"In other words, the income account should be prepared on the basis of cash receipts and disbursements notwithstanding the fact that a creature of the Government itself—the Interstate Commerce Commission—especially provides that the methods to be pursued by the railroads in ascertaining their income shall not be on this basis but on the basis of income accrued and expenses incurred. Yet it does not appear that it occurred to any of our representatives in passing the bill, or to the President in signing it, that there was any inconsistency.

"The point is that such inconsistency would have been apparent at once to a certified public accountant if he had had anything to do with drafting the bill. Moreover, the bill would have been logically arranged and so clearly presented as to render unnecessary the flood of rulings by the Commissioner of Internal Revenue.

"Numerous illustrations might be given of cases in which points of controversy could have been quickly and practically cleared away by a public accountant, whose decisions in matters involving the proper classification of investments, assets, and income would be consistent with the purposes of the profession which, in the discharge of its functions, deals only with conditions, facts, and figures—it has no place for bias, perversions, fancies, or narrow and contracted view-points; on the contrary, it calls for breadth of vision, discretion, tact, and diplomacy."

The following are extracts from press comments which appeared after the publication of the address on "Publicity of Financial Affairs of Corporations":

A timely hint to corporations. How they can check the muck-rakers. The muck-raker depends upon the ignorance and credulity of the people regarding the workings of corporations.

He misleads or falsifies, trusting to the ignorance and credulity of his reader. Unfortunately, the corporations assailed do not defend themselves and hence are laid open to the charge either of thus acknowledging their guilt, or thus displaying their fear of publicity, or, in other words, their cowardice. The world loves a fighter, hence the mistake of the corporations. Mr. Sells proposes to have the corporation through the common channels of publicity tell the public the truth. His method is certainly worth considering and is strongly sustained by an admirable argument and statement of facts.

*Leslie's Illustrated Weekly,* New York.

Thoughtful address—it is well that Mr. Sells has called attention so clearly to the necessity for relief. He speaks impartially as becomes a public accountant and no man who knows him will accuse him of bias.... A copy of his address should be in the hands of every corporation official. The remedy which Mr. Sells suggests is the only one possible if corporations are to continue operation under restricted management.... Mr. Sells is absolutely right.

*The Journal of Accountancy,* New York.

# XI

# CORPORATE MANAGEMENT COMPARED WITH GOVERNMENT CONTROL

# XI

# CORPORATE MANAGEMENT COMPARED WITH GOVERNMENT CONTROL[1]

Accountants' knowledge of corporate affairs is intimate, accurate, and substantially complete. Management of corporations is generally intelligent and economical. Management of Government bureaus is generally loose, irregular, and dishonest. Comparisons of corporate and Government administration. Development of railways under Government regulation and business under private control. Graphic illustration showing comparison of railway, agricultural, and pig iron development, and bank clearings and deposits in the United States.

EDITORIAL NOTE: Observations from letters pertaining to subject. Tendency toward Government regulation of business. Political despotism versus public welfare. Press comments.

THE Society of Certified Public Accountants of the State of New Jersey is especially conspicuous because more corporations and more corporate capital have their corporate home in the state of New Jersey than in any other state. And so I want to take this occasion to discuss, and in a spirit that shall lack neither candor nor courage, certain public questions upon which the experience of a public accountant is competent to throw light.

The position of the public accountant in respect to corporations and their management is always an independent one. Unlike the attorney he is not ex-

[1] Response to a toast, "The American Association of Public Accountants," at the banquet of the Society of Certified Public Accountants of the State of New Jersey, on its tenth anniversary, Newark, New Jersey, January 20, 1908.

pected to make out a case. The character of the service he renders is impersonal. All he can do is to tell what the facts are, and they exist for his examination in forms so tangible and so subject to other scrutiny than his own that even if he were willing to prostitute his calling he would never dare to do so. It is equally true that the knowledge he obtains of the affairs of corporations is necessarily intimate, accurate, and substantially complete.

Our country just now is passing through a period of acute financial stringency. The securities representing its properties are selling at prices that range from 30% to 60% lower than were obtained for them one year ago. The money needed to keep business going is harder to get today than was any sum, however great, for the extension and development of business one year ago, and the questions, What is the matter? How has this come about? Who is responsible? are on everybody's tongue. The answers that are so generously provided seem to me very wide of the mark. Usually they involve grave reflections upon corporate management, and usually they come from a class of people who are particularly glib with their tongue, or ready with their pen, and who seem to have no other qualification for throwing light upon so grave a problem.

We are told that the corporation managers are dishonest; that they "exploit" the people and their utilities; that they put their own enrichment above their duty to the stockholding interest or to the patronizing public; and that before there can be a return of the splendid prosperity we were enjoying, the corporation must be regulated and the Government must step in with a sharp eye and a big stick.

My experience in the conduct of independent and impartial examinations of books of account and affairs has covered many years and has been concerned with the Federal Government, state governments, and city governments. It has covered the field also of railway, street railway, light, power, and other public service corporations. It has dealt with industrial corporations, the so-called "trusts." It has taken me into banks, trust companies, and insurance companies; into educational and charitable institutions. I think I may say it has taken me pretty generally over the whole field of public and private business, and if I am to judge by what my eyes have seen, it is the unassailable truth that almost any one of the men who stand at the head of our great business institutions is far more competent to run the Government, and would run it more economically, more wisely, and more honestly than any of those who are in the business of running governments.

I know as a matter of fact that the management of our great properties is generally intelligent and economical, and that the management of our Government bureaus is generally loose, irregular, and frequently dishonest; and when I read the articles with which so many of our newspapers and magazines are filled nowadays, reflecting on the men whose genius is developing the country's resources, and when I hear the proposals of politicians, from the most eminent to the least, for the passage of laws to hamper and restrict the energies of these men on the theory that their integrity is open to suspicion, my mind inevitably brings up the contrast that I always observe between a corporation's way of doing things and a government's, as disclosed by their respective records and books of account.

For the purpose of this comparison, incompetency and dishonesty need not be separated. Putting them together it is my deliberate estimate, that, judged by the highest standards prevailing in the best conducted corporations, there is less than 10% of both among men in the management of corporations generally, and at least 90% of both among public officeholders, and I base this estimate upon my experience as a public accountant.

The men entrusted with the management of the corporations are better fitted to administer the affairs of such corporations and to exercise judgment in matters concerning both the investor and the public which takes their product or utilizes their franchises, than are those men who hold public office qualified to fill even their own positions, much less to undertake administrative control over corporations. The facts that prove this do not deal with the mere matter of honesty and efficiency. The organization of a public bureau is much less compact, much less harmonious in its operation than the organization of a great railway or a great industrial corporation. The men at the head of such business organizations, in practically every case, are experts, working diligently, in harmony, and ready to work to the limit of their endurance, with full and direct control of their subordinates. On the other hand, nothing can be more notorious, the results are obvious to every public accountant who investigates, than the fact that in nine cases out of ten the head of a public department spends most of his time promoting his political interests, and the employees generally, protected by the civil service regulations, are looking to see how little rather than how much work they can get into their appointed short hours.

We are not without information of the effects upon great business industries of being hampered by Government regulations, as compared with the effect of being let alone. It is rare, of course, that conditions common to a great business are due to a single cause, but in this instance the signs point that way.

The two greatest business interests of the country are represented by the railways and by agriculture, and they are particularly interrelated. Everything that tends to restrain capital from investing in railway enterprises; everything that holds back the extension of railway enterprises into new and undeveloped country checks the settlement of new farms and the production of new crops. The manufacturer, on the other hand, finds his interests facilitated by the erection of his factories and shops in old and closely settled communities where the transportation problem is already fully solved. So, note the comparison.

In addition to a vast amount of state legislation in restraint of railways that began at about the time the Interstate Commerce Act was passed in 1887, that evil enactment, with its subsequent amendments, ushered in the era of restriction and introduced the period of railway persecution by law. Prior to that time railway construction had progressed in line with the development of business generally, but since that day, notwithstanding the enormous increase of capital resources, the railway industry has fallen far below other lines of development, and with it also have fallen the principal agricultural interests.

From 1878 to 1887 the average number of miles of railways constructed per annum was 7,013, but in the 10 years following the passage of this Act, the average was only 3,537, or a falling off of about 50%. A normal growth since 1887, to keep pace with the development of industries generally, should show an average in excess of that which had distinguished the earlier period. No less than 12,876 miles of railway were constructed in the very year, 1887, in which the Interstate Commerce Act was passed; since that time the largest year of construction was in the year following, 1888, when the total was only 6,900 miles. The total mileage at the end of 1887 was 149,214; at the close of 1906 the total mileage was 222,635, an increase during these 19 years of only 49%, while in the preceding 19 years the increase had been 253%.

The explanation of this condition of things is not to be found in the suggestion that the country has been occupied. In the region west of the Mississippi, as suitable for development as any country through which any of the transcontinental lines were built, there were in 1904, outside of Alaska and Texas, no fewer than 473,836,000 acres of unoccupied public lands, while in Texas one-half of the area, or fully 84,000,000 acres, has not yet been penetrated by lines of railway. In the region west of the Mississippi, where there is only a little over 100,000 miles of road, there is an area at the present time sufficient to support at least 50% more railway mileage.

Note now the figures showing the development of businesses which have not been hampered by that sort of Government regulation which hinders their management and frightens their investors.

National and state bank deposits increased from $1,737,000,000 in 1888 to $6,941,000,000 in 1906, or in the enormous measure of 299%; bank clearings increased from $49,098,000,000 to $159,808,000,000, or 225%; and the production of pig iron from 7,268,000 tons to 28,280,000 tons, or 289%. The Lake Superior iron ore shipments increased from 9,000,000 tons in 1890, the figures showing the tons shipped in 1888 were not available, to 38,500,000 tons in 1906, or 324%. The statistics of manufactures for the period from 1888 to 1906 are not available, but for the 10 years from 1890 to 1900 the capital invested in manufactures had increased from $6,525,-

000,000 to $9,835,000,000, or 50%; but the capital invested in railways had increased during those 10 years from $10,021,000,000 to $11,892,000,000, or only in the measure of 18%, with a mileage in the measure of 16%.

The fact that the causes, whatever they are, which have throttled railway development, are also responsible for holding back the development of agriculture appears clearly enough in the fact that agriculture is the only other large industry which has not developed in proportion with the production of raw material, the growth of manufactures, and the increase of banking resources.

Since the time when the Egyptian people began the system of rotating crops, agriculture has been the greatest source of national enrichment, and doubtless the greatest factor in the civilization of the world.

With all the lands that are available in this country still to be reached by railway construction, and with unlimited markets abroad for our agricultural products, the production of corn, wheat, and cotton increased not at all in keeping with other developments, but only approximately with the progress of railway development.

In the period from 1888 to 1906, the increase in the production of corn was from 1,988,000,000 bushels to 2,927,000,000 bushels, or only 47%; that of wheat was from 416,000,000 bushels to 735,000,000 bushels, or only 77%; while that of cotton was from 6,941,000 bales to 13,290,000 bales, or only 91%; and the fact that cotton did better than wheat or corn is accounted for by the reinvigoration of the South.

It is interesting also to note that the revenue to the investor from his interests in railways is far less than his revenue from an interest in manufactures. The average rate of net income on railway investments is only about 4%, while the average net income from investments in manufactures is about 15%.

I want to quote, and with earnest approval, the language employed by President Hadley of Yale University, in a lecture on "Ethics of Corporation Management," delivered in the latter part of 1906:

> Personally, I am one of those who look with serious distrust on each extension of political activity. I believe that the Interstate Commerce Law did more to prevent wise railroad regulation than any other event in the history of the country. I think that the Courts would have dealt with our industrial problems better than they have done if the Anti-Trust Act had never been passed. I have gravely doubted the wisdom of some of the more recent measures passed by the National Government.

The prejudice that has been aroused against the men who have written their names largest upon the geography of their country by railway construction and development, or whose genius has built up such corporate organizations as exist in steel, in oil, in the telegraph, and in other lines of industry; the prejudice that swept over the West in the days of Populism, and that now seems so far to dictate the policies of both the great political parties that their old-time controversies are forgotten and they are merged in attacks upon the business of the country, is a prejudice that is based upon two false assumptions; first, that the men of great affairs are lacking in integrity, and, second, that the men of small affairs are oversupplied with it. I shall not say that the reverse is more nearly true, but I do say that almost every instance of great success in this country is an example of a combination, in the man who has accomplished it, of scrupulous honesty, great frugality of personal expenditure during the years of struggle, and unbounded industry; while as a commentary upon general good conduct of the masses as such, it is a pertinent remark that if during the last few years one of our largest street railway systems could have gathered into its treasury all the fares that were passed up to its conductors, together with all the fares for which it gave rides but for which the passengers had contrived to omit to pay, it would not now be in the hands of receivers.

The loss to traction lines in all principal cities by the evasion and the dodging of passengers, and by the misconduct of conductors, is estimated at from 5% to 10% of their gross earnings. The aggregate loss to shareholders of traction companies throughout the country must amount to a great many millions of dollars annually.

Christian Socialism, the equal protection of the individual rights of all, the doctrine of the Golden Rule, is the only sort of socialism that should exist in a free country where each man's endowment of industry and ability should be permitted to achieve for him that full measure of success of which it is capable.

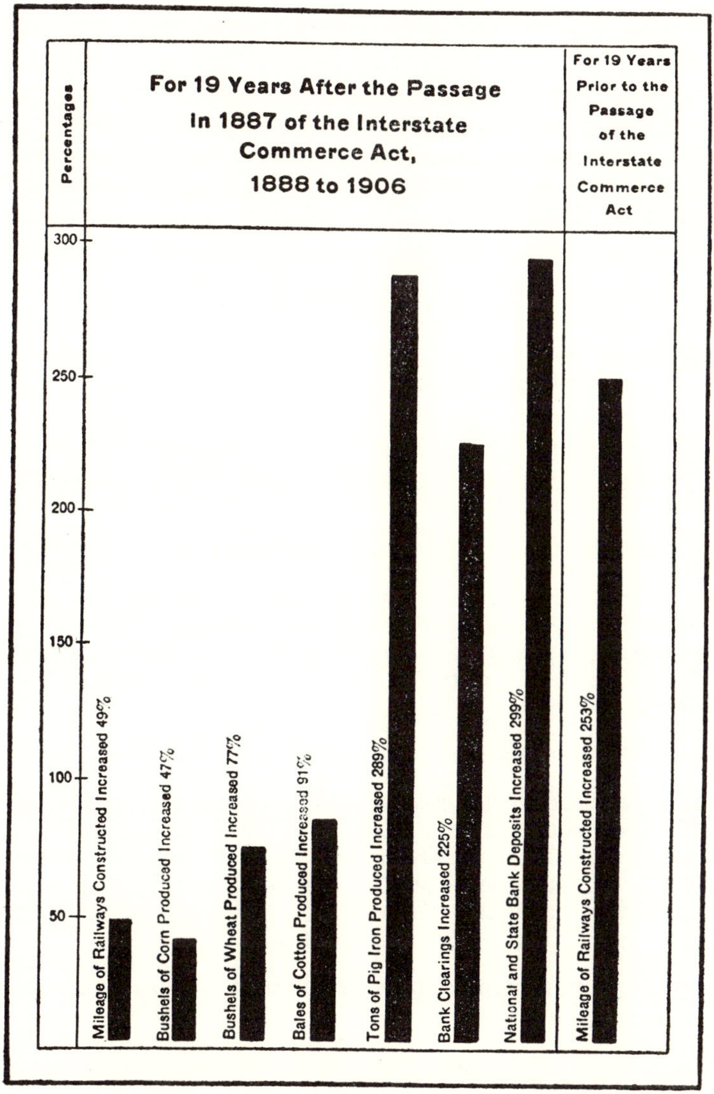


Comparison of Railway, Agriculture, and Pig-Iron Development, and Bank Clearings and Deposits in the United States.

EDITORIAL NOTE: This enunciation called forth more comment, by far, than any other public utterance of the author. The comments were, with two or three exceptions, not only favorable but extremely congratulatory. Letters by the score were received from men prominent in every walk of life: business men, bankers, lawyers, railroad officials; all except Government employees. Many were willing to applaud. No one who was informed, however, apparently had the gift of discernment necessary to see the situation in its true light, or, if so, the courage to give voice thereto. One politician acknowledged the truth of the indictment, but admitted that it would have been too much to expect that anyone concerned with the Government service or its law-making would have the courage, for political reasons, to point out the true situation.

A prominent San Francisco banker wrote:

> If men like you would have the time to fill the columns of the newspapers of the United States instead of the men you designate as anxious to fill space at so much a line, the education of the public in the right direction would be much easier than it is today.

The following came from a leading New York lawyer:

> From the extracts I have seen of your remarks, they are what the Indians used to call, when we had any real Indians, "good medicine," and the community at large will be benefited by reading what you have to say, especially as it is based upon the intelligent observation of what you have seen on the inside of so much of our great corporations.

The senior member of a well-known law firm in Kansas City said:

> It contains huge chunks of cold, unadulterated truth, and altogether is the sanest and most useful public utterance that I know of within the past four years.

The reaction of an outstanding university educator is summed up in the following:

> I have rarely seen in so short a compass so vigorous an exposure of the evils of tinkering by politicians, eager for the applause and the votes of the hysterical multitude, with things that they do not understand. If we considered the general welfare of the country at large, it is, in my opinion, unquestionably true that the meddling of incompetent legislators has done far more harm than the occasional rascality of leading railway and business men.

In addition to being quoted and reproduced extensively in the press, there were wide-spread and voluminous requests for copies of the speech. One railroad company asked for a thousand copies, to be distributed among employees. It was reproduced in its entirety by several trade publications. The reproduction in pamphlet form ran to five editions.

Mr. Sells' pronouncement was the original public presentation of the matter. It was suggested to him by a call from the London correspondent of the *New York Times,* who, on the occasion of one of Mr. Sells' visits to London, approached him for an opinion with regard to the conditions in America during the latter part of the year 1907. This, it will be recalled, was the year of the money panic. There was not only much concern over recovery from the serious depression, but considerable criticism of certain individuals who had stood high in the financial world. This attitude was stimulated, if not in large part occasioned, by the policy of the Government toward corporations, a disposition to indulge in what was then called "muck-raking," and the threat to wield the "big stick" on corporations.

If Mr. Sells' conclusions, derived from a comparison of corporate management with Government control, were correct in 1908, present-day comparison must, it seems, inevitably result in a conclusion much more pronounced. The Interstate Commerce Commission has surrendered none of its power; if anything, that power has been increased. In many directions Government control has extended its grasp until corporate management has, in numerous instances, been driven to the brink of despair. Railroads are still gasping from the near-death blow administered during the war. It is only necessary to compare their operating results in 1922 with those of the industrials, to be assured on this point. Coal mining is threatened with Government regulation. Corporations and individuals are still staggering from the burden of taxation. Constructive legislation, based on sound business principles, is constantly hampered by the greed of politicians. One has only to look at the record of congressional convention during the past year to have little doubt about this matter.

While optimism preaches the doctrine that "God is in His Heaven, and all's well with the world," it is nevertheless a serious reflection on the national common sense of the American people that they have permitted the situation to develop to the present point where more or less everything in the way of progress is blocked by political interference and strife. The fate of the League of Nations and the Ship Subsidy Bill are cases in point. Regard for the country's needs must always be subserved, it seems, to party consideration.

National consciousness and strong leadership are needed now perhaps as much as at any other time in the history of the country. May the reproduction of Mr. Sells' striking arraignment contribute something to the furtherance of the efforts put forth by the national chief executive in attempting to correct the situation.

Extracts from press comments on the original publication follow:

In an address.... Elijah W. Sells, of the accounting firm of Haskins & Sells.... made some interesting and pertinent remarks bearing upon the management of railroad and other corporations and those who direct their affairs. He contrasted corporate management with Government management. By reason of his profession, Mr. Sells is well qualified to speak on this subject. He has had unusual opportunities for observation and for getting at the actual facts, on which alone a correct judgment can be based....

Altogether, Mr. Sells, it will be seen, has succeeded in crowding many facts and much solid truth into his remarks, and the address, coming from such a well-informed public accountant, must be considered as forming an important contribution to the discussions of the subject.

*The Commercial and Financial Chronicle,* New York.

.... Mr. Elijah W. Sells, the well-known public accountant, has given the public much food for thought in a comparison which he draws between the management of Government bureaus and of the various classes of public service, industrial, and business corporations, a comparison which he is peculiarly fitted to make from his life-long experience.

*The Banking Law Journal,* New York.

# XII

# WHY NOT LESSEN THE EVILS OF PRESENT TAXATION?

XII

# WHY NOT LESSEN THE EVILS OF PRESENT TAXATION?[1]

Accountants peculiarly fitted to pass judgment on taxation. Present income tax, surtax, and excess profits tax and their iniquitous results. American tax method compared with British. Remedies. Advantages.

EDITORIAL NOTE: Lack of Government cooperation with recognized experts. Necessity for taxation. Present pending legislation. Desirability of releasing funds tied up in tax-exempt securities for business expansion. Authority for taxing all incomes contained in sixteenth amendment to Constitution.

TAXES we have eternally with us. They are the price we pay for civilization, organization, government. They began under the regime of Moses, starting with a 10% income tax called "tithes." Taxation in some form has never left the earth since that time.

While much has been written and said upon the subject of taxation and possible revision, it is still far from settled and there is apparently room for discussion.

Public accountants are peculiarly fitted to pass judgment on the subject of taxation. They touch every phase and problem of business in some way and are also familiar with the affairs of government, federal, state, and municipal. They perceive, at close range, the effect of taxation on business and the great

[1] A paper read before the Accountants' Club, Hotel McAlpin, New York, July 13, 1921.

disturbance which it causes. Better than any other class do they know the superior excellence, economy, and efficiency of the management of business as compared with that of government and the far-reaching meritorious effect of business upon all interests.

The practice of my own firm has taken us during the past year into the affairs of several thousand concerns, and much of our work has involved tax problems from so many angles that it has forced on us conclusions as to present methods and needs. This is typical of all practicing public accountants.

To run the government of a nation, state or city, requires money, and the bulk of that money can come only through taxation. The greater the amount of funds required the greater the amount that must be furnished by the people. This we accept as self-evident, natural, inevitable. But we have a right to demand, and a duty to make our demand vigorous and insistent, that the basis of that taxation be wisely considered, fair and equitable, aimed at no one class, the tax widely distributed, and arranged so that it fulfils its purpose with the minimum disturbance of business and the welfare of the individual.

The present federal income tax, with its surtax for individuals and its excess profits tax for corporations, is flagrantly unfair, inequitable and fulfils its purpose with the maximum disturbance of business and the welfare of the individual. During the war loyal citizens faced it cheerfully, accepting its discrimination and injustice as a minor matter in the dark shadows of a world tragedy. They took it as but another of the necessary evils of war. But they are now rightly and insistently registering their protest against its continuance, with its bad features unchanged, as an unnecessary evil in time of peace and as disturbing, disheartening, and destructive to business activity and enterprise.

Business is the very life-blood of the nation. It employs labor, pays its bills, adds to the wealth and influence of the country, and keeps money in circulation. Whatever drains business of its resources dulls its initiative, saps its vitality and holds the nation back from reconstruction and sane, normal progress. The Government's just need of money does not essentially make right its method of getting it.

The present income tax, and its twin incumbrances, the surtax and the excess profits tax, are wrong because they cripple unnaturally individual and corporate enterprise and activity at the very hour when they are most needed. When a patient is slowly convalescing from the severe shock of a long, hard, weakening illness in which he may have lost much blood it is not an auspicious time to bleed him further. This is precisely what is being done to business by the Government in the name of taxes.

Since we entered the war we have heard constantly of thrift. It has been dinned into our ears by thousands of speakers, has been flaunted at us in our morning papers, and has been relentlessly billboarded and placarded into our consciousness as one of the supreme duties of life. As a war measure it was a needed and inspiring call. Thrift was a supreme duty then. It is a great duty now and always.

There are two phases of thrift that must be printed in red letters for Congress to read in relation to our taxes. Let the Government today, no matter what it did during the war, practice the thrift it preached to the people. Let it take its own medicine, eliminate the waste, the extravagance, the reckless administration, the appalling expenditure in bills which appeal to certain classes and that have in them more practical politics than practical patriotism. Let Congress realize that even a billion dollars is worth saving and exercise some of this thrift. Such a course would reduce the demands of the tax, put us in a better position to pay what we have to pay and make the paying easier. The other present lesson in thrift is for the Government to learn to save the business of the nation instead of losing it by sapping its substance; save business so that business may save enough to pay its taxes.

The individual is encouraged to be thrifty, to "lay something up for a rainy day." A corporation should do the same, since a good year may precede one or more bad ones and the accumulated reserve may be needed to make up the deficit of the poorer years. But most of all, business should save for its rehabilitation and further expansion.

The iniquitous excess profits tax and surtaxes are uneconomic in that they stimulate extravagance and reckless expenditures in many ways instead of inspiring thrift. Many businesses have used advertising space beyond their real needs, have been willing to pay unnecessarily high prices for labor, and have plunged into expenses that ordinary business wisdom would not sanction under normal conditions, thereby intensifying an already abnormal condition. Taxes are responsible for these extravagances.

The Government Loan Organization is advertising for the "Legion of Dollar Savers" (a squad in every home) to invest their savings in the future of the United States of America and says: "Business will boom and factories reopen—but more money will be needed to enable the wheels of industry and commerce to turn at full speed.... Dollars invested through this channel will ultimately promote business enterprise and provide employment for all."

While these few dollars saved and added to business are desirable it is more essential to conserve and protect the billions of dollars that are now in business. The Government should recognize the rights of the large interests not as against those less prosperous, but in order that there may be cooperation between them in the resuscitation of business and the promotion of its further progress.

Fostering the interests of those who have billions now invested in business will "promote business enterprise and provide employment for all" with greater rapidity than can be hoped to be accomplished by the Government's invitation to the Legion of Dollar

Savers to subscribe dollars in small quantities, commendable as that may be.

Moreover, those of the Legion of Dollar Savers who have the requisite character and capacity will, if they respond to the Government's call, soon find themselves in the same position as that in which the large investors are today, because the small investors are in exactly the same position today as were the large investors only a few years ago.

During the last two years millions have been withdrawn from business by those in the higher groups of profits and disposed of among those less successful, in such instalments as to keep the latter out of the high brackets of profits, and make the tax resulting less than they receive in cash distribution. So much of the value of these interests as could be paid for in cash has been reinvested in non-taxable municipal, state, and county bonds. There have also been millions in securities, belonging to those having large holdings, disposed of and the proceeds likewise reinvested in non-taxable bonds. The aggregate of these processes makes an enormous drain upon business resources. But there are other evils. Investment in the non-taxable bonds has encouraged extravagance in municipal, state, and county expenditures with increasing debts and high interest for the future. This has brought about high prices for labor and materials and has had a tendency to interfere with needed housing operations at reasonable prices.

In many cases those having large invested interests have actually given away millions to members of their families and others in order that the aggregate of the taxation for the estate may be lessened.

The law defeats its very purpose by causing a decline in excess profits and surtaxes from these various sources.

Note an example of the cramping and paralyzing effect of this taxation. If a partnership undertakes to save one-half of its year's profits for the capital necessary to take care of its future needs and expansion, and one member's share of the profits amounts to a quarter of a million dollars, he will at the present rate have to obtain outside of his business $1,670 in order to pay his federal income tax and surtax amounting to $126,670. Thus he would have to pay more than he actually received in money out of the business, to say nothing of providing for his state income tax, his real estate tax, if he is fortunate enough to own his own home, or other taxable property and all the expenses incidental to domestic and other needs.

This is typical of countless other instances of the injustice and the inequity of the present taxation. It is an un-American tax and does not fit in with the spirit or needs of our people. It was modeled on the income tax of Europe where conditions were different from those of this country at the time of its enactment. In Europe were many large entailed estates, the heirs to which had little or no relation to business, while in this country both the money and those who inherit it or make it are actively engaged in business. In Europe the income tax does little harm and is but a slight disturbing factor. The British Government developed a plan of taxation on the average of three years' income which is a better basis for establishing a nearer approach to equilibrium in government revenue. In America the income tax does more harm with less justification for its being. But this income tax is with us and is likely to remain. We must accept its bad principles but modify its terms.

What should be done and without delay is threefold: First, eliminate the surtax and the excess profits tax; second, reduce the present income tax rate; third, provide in their place a new tax which will yield the needed revenue with the least possible disturbance of business, whether corporate, partnership, or individual.

A tax that would apply only upon sales to the consumer and would not be made on sales of raw materials, partly manufactured articles sold to manufacturers, or on products sold to jobbers for resale, would be just and equitable.

The tax on consumption to be paid by the consumer, with the word "consumption" broadly construed, should be a uniform rate for each of the various lines or grades, starting with a small percentage on necessities and articles in common use and graded up to a high rate for luxuries. With no serious disturbance to any business, it would produce billions annually for the Government's needs.

This form of taxation would have many advantages:

1. It would give wider distribution so that all classes would pay and being in small amounts would not be a drain on the finances of any.

2. Being paid at the time of sale, the likelihood of tax evasion would be lessened and as a "pay as you buy" tax would be paid in trifling sums as a finality, instead of being massed as a large amount to be paid later.

3. It would tend to stabilize prices to the consumer and eliminate excessive profits that in many cases are intended to anticipate undetermined taxes. There would be no incentive for the dealer to avoid payment as it would be collected from others and held apart for that purpose.

4. It would be a genuine encouragement to economy and thrift because the bulk of the taxes would fall upon expenditures and not upon profits that are accumulated. It would place no limits or determents to what an individual, partnership, or corporation might make or save.

5. Taxation on spending, not on earning, applied in large measures and distributed against all who make expenditures would be logical, safe, and equitable. It would give the individual the largest measure of freedom in his financial affairs.

6. It would be a simple form and relatively easy of

administration. It would be computed mostly by business houses equipped to keep records and perform this service economically and efficiently. The stamp tax plan could be applied to the small businesses.

Taxation based upon consumption with varying rates, from the minimum for the necessities to the maximum for the luxuries, is not unlike the principle applied to the tariff which this Government adopted at the beginning and has continued to the present time, varying only as party politics made the rate high or low.

We must recognize that our Government is going on for many years to come expending billions for civil operations and armament, part of which may be needless and unwise, in addition to the interest on war debts and their ultimate redemption. The American people must see the problem of raising revenue by taxation with broad, clear vision and with practical, not theoretical, knowledge of business and its needs. A Congress which ignores the needs of business invites further industrial calamity and economic discord that is far reaching. Just as surely as discrimination against small incomes is reprehensible so is that against large incomes. What is needed is not favoritism to either, but justice to both. The interests of business and the interests of the country generally are identical. The prosperity of the one means the prosperity of the other. Any injustice or other cause which hampers business affects adversely the whole country and all of the people.

Editorial Note: Mr. Sells has built up an exceedingly strong case in support of a proposed sales tax plan. His varied experience in connection with the financial phases of industrial and governmental activities qualifies him admirably to discuss this subject in an impartial and intelligent manner. Unfortunately, however, there are too many of our legislators who have in mind solely their own political and selfish interests and who only too often turn a deaf ear to really constructive programs of legislation. This vicious condition necessarily invites corruption and is attended by destructive results. But just so long as congressmen refuse to accept the opinions and recommendations of recognized experts, then just so long will this condition continue.

As an example of this flagrant practice, one may recall what happened to the Mellon plan for tax reduction when it was placed before Congress for action. Volumes of opposition flamed forth from the various political factions. When the plan was finally adopted it was so different from the original that many of the practical benefits were sacrificed. Yet, Mr. Mellon, from his varied experience in the world of finance and from his knowledge of the operations of the United States Treasury, was probably more competent than any other person to formulate the method that could best be employed. The changes, all of which were without merit, were in answer to the demands of cliques and blocs which were more anxious to obstruct than to cooperate.

Awakening the public, however, to the seriousness of such a matter is not an easy task. The public is too heterogeneous a mass and too unfamiliar and disinterested in the affairs of government to be in a position where it could vigorously demand that politicians subserve their interests to those of the public. Perhaps, through a process of education the day will come when voters will give as much attention to government as they now give to the selection of their personal needs. The politician will then be made to feel his responsibility, and he will be called upon to justify the confidence which his constituents place in him.

In the meantime, we shall be confronted with such problems as that of taxes. At present everybody concedes that taxes are too high. It is probably not too sweeping a statement to say that everyone would like to have taxes reduced. But taxes furnish the means whereby the expenses of government are met, and no one expects any Federal Government, or subdivision thereof, to operate without funds.

The time-worn question of how much any government properly requires for necessary expenses may never be answered. This country of ours, however, has put itself in the sound position of budgeting its financial affairs, and the machinery has been provided for estimating in advance, with a fair degree of precision, the expense of conducting government. This development has occurred subsequent to the date of Mr. Sells' article.

Based on past experience and profitable future needs, the Secretary of the Treasury, Mr. Mellon, has explained that present rates of taxation may be substantially reduced. Certain politicians have tried to relate the issue of tax reduction to the soldiers' bonus. Others have, however, raised questions which have an economic rather than a political aspect. They believe, with Mr. Mellon and Mr. Sells, that a reduction of surtaxes would tend to attract back into industry funds which have been diverted therefrom by tax-exempt securities. They claim that municipal, county, and state projects are as much industry as the business operations carried on by private enterprises and the argument may not be readily controverted.

In addition, we find linked with tax-exempt securities the principle of "easy come, easy go." This naturally tends to extravagance, or at least to the utilization of funds beyond the point of necessity and economic desirability, and, apparently, without the realization that interest on funds borrowed for local improvements and sinking-fund payments must be met by local taxation. The elimination of the tax-exempt feature of securities would, in these cases, cause the burden of taxation to be shifted from the people as a whole to those who happened to live in localities where extravagant public improvements were under way.

Furthermore, if an amendment to the Constitution were to prohibit the issue of tax-exempt securities, then all securities, both industrial and municipal, would, so far as surtaxes are concerned, be on the same basis. Accordingly, the taxpayer of large means seeking investment would be in the position of choosing between industrials and municipals, having in mind the advantages of the respective bonds with regard to security of principal and interest return. Municipals would then be obliged to compete with industrials. The tendency of local taxpayers would probably be to object to issues which would carry high rates of interest and local extravagances would tend toward curtailment. In all likelihood, industrials would be in a better position to offer higher rates, and would, therefore, attract available capital.

Amendment to the Constitution would perhaps accomplish the same thing which Mr. Mellon hopes to accomplish by reducing surtaxes, namely, the attraction of additional capital to the essential industries. But why amend the Constitution again? The sixteenth amendment provides as follows:

> The Congress shall have the power to lay and collect taxes on incomes from whatever source derived, without

apportionment among the several states and without regard to any census or enumeration.

No authority to tax income from municipal, county, and state securities could be more specific. Its application should be availed of immediately.

# XIII

# A PLAN FOR INTERNATIONAL PEACE

# XIII

## A PLAN FOR INTERNATIONAL PEACE[1]

Tangible and intangible costs of war. Precepts that should receive agreement among nations of the world. Election of representatives who constitute peace tribunal. Estimated expenditures and savings that would result. Proposed land and sea forces. Tabulation showing approximate population, number of men, and cost per annum of armies and navies on peace basis of practically all nations; and estimated number of men in armies, and number of representatives under proposed plan of a world's peace tribunal.

Editorial Note: Inadequacy of power in the Hague Tribunal. Lack of power in proposed League of Nations. Mr. Sells' plan developed from a business rather than a legal or political standpoint.

The war now being waged, the greatest in history, brings vividly to the mind the need, when peace again is established, for some definite plan whereby to insure its permanency throughout the world. Aghast at the struggle in which many nations are involved, humanity is disheartened over the failure of peace plans heretofore proposed, and hopeful that the time draws near when the nations of the world will find and adopt some plan to secure all people in the peaceful pursuit of their respective undertakings against interruption by international warfare.

It has been said that war stimulates manhood and makes for strength of character. While this may be true, such benefits sink into insignificance when com-

[1] An address at the meeting of the New York State Society of Certified Public Accountants, New York, Monday, January 11, 1915.

pared with the enormous drains that war makes upon the social fabric and the world's wealth arising from: (1) loss of life; (2) disability of survivors; (3) suffering of dependents; (4) distress of non-participants; (5) destruction of property; (6) damage to commerce; and (7) taxation of the cost.

The overwhelming magnitude of each of these products of warfare, all forcefully illustrated by the present European conflict, has been so extensively brought to public notice that there is no need for amplification by discussion.

The many peace expressions coming from the powers in recent years have indicated the need for a practicable plan that will permanently prevent warfare between nations. Mere conventions between nations will not accomplish permanent peace; this must come through irrevocable compact providing for something substantially effective. I believe the solution of this question lies in the establishment of an independent tribunal endowed with the right to adjudicate international differences and provided with the power to enforce its decisions.

In order that such a tribunal may be able to accomplish this the nations must grant to it unqualified authority to organize for efficiently carrying out the objects of its formation, must transfer their navies to the tribunal, must reduce their armies, and must be committed to and make regular appropriations of the funds necessary for the tribunal's maintenance.

In the interest of humanity I am encouraged to

present a plan, convinced of its feasibility and hopeful of its adoption, if it can have the approval of our own nation and a potential presentation to other nations at the proper time.

*The full agreement between the nations of the world should include the following general precepts:*

### Precept Number 1

The constitution of a world's peace tribunal to which shall be referred all differences between nations which cannot be settled amicably by themselves, and the irrevocable delegation to such tribunal: First, of authority to adjudicate such differences; Second, of power to enforce its decisions after due notice has been given the nations in interest; Third, of power to suppress hostilities between nations arising from any cause whatsoever, and to compel them to submit their differences to the tribunal for adjudication; and Fourth, of power to enforce these precepts.

### Precept Number 2

The requirements imposed upon the nations shall be: First, to cede and transfer to the tribunal, without reservation, all war-ships and other naval equipment and discontinue all navy yards and all other related establishments except such as may be needed for the purposes of the tribunal and which shall be ceded to it; Second, to dismantle and raze all fortifications except those needed for the tribunal which shall be ceded and transferred to it, together with all munitions of war except such of the small ordnance as may be necessary for the nations' armies; Third, to reduce all armies to a basis of internal necessities, approximately 50% of the armies as they exist on a peace basis and not to exceed 1/20 of 1% of the nations' population for standing armies, and no larger force of reserves or militia for principalities or state subdivisions, with corresponding reduction in military equipment and munitions and in arsenals or plants for their manufacture, and, in the case of factories not under the control of governments, limitation by law to the manufacture of small arms in quantities not to exceed national requirements; and Fourth, to confine the operations of armies of the nations to their respective territories.

### Precept Number 3

The annual appropriation by each nation for 25 years, for the support of the tribunal, of one-third of the average annual expenditures for the army and navy for the past 5 years, to be paid to the treasurer of the tribunal.

### Precept Number 4

The annual appointment or election by every nation of a representative or representatives to a congress of the peace tribunal to meet on the first Monday of June and adjourn not later than the last Saturday of September in each year, one representative from each nation with a population of 25,000,000 or less, two from each nation with a population between 25,000,000 and 100,000,000, three from each nation with a population between 100,000,000 and 250,000,000, and four from each nation with a population in excess of 250,000,000; such representatives to be subject to reappointment or reelection for not more than three years continuously, but thereafter to be eligible for reappointment or reelection only upon the lapse of one year.

### Precept Number 5

That the congress upon organization shall be authorized and required: To create three departments of nine members each for the conduct of the affairs of the tribunal, viz.; a judiciary to include a chief justice; a civil commission to include a chairman, a secretary, a treasurer, and a comptroller; and an armament commission to include a chairman and a chief of armaments; and to elect from among its numbers the members of each department, and to administer to them appropriate oaths of office.

### Precept Number 6

That the congress shall be authorized and required to make appropriations for the expenses of its first session and for the expenses of the tribunal for its first fiscal year which shall begin

October 1 and end September 30, and that annually thereafter it shall make appropriations upon budgets submitted by the civil and armament commissions for the annual expenses of the tribunal.

### PRECEPT NUMBER 7

That the members of the departments be elected separately by ballot; that originally there be elected one of each department for nine years, one of each department for eight years, and so on, to one of each department for one year, and each year thereafter one of each department for nine years to hold office commencing October 1 following; that not more than one member of any one department shall be from the same nation, and that no member shall be eligible for reelection to any department before the lapse of three years or to membership in the congress during the period of his incumbency; that nominations shall be made on or before July 1 and shall be voted upon not later than August 20, and that nominations shall be made at least ten days before voting takes place; that the chairman of the congress shall appoint three tellers of election, each from a different country, who will count the ballots and report to the congress, and the chairman of the congress shall declare elected the nominee receiving a plurality, and in event of a tie the election shall be determined by lot, the chairman of the congress to appoint a committee of three (not the tellers), each from a different country, to determine the lot.

### Precept Number 8

That any member of any department may be impeached and removed for malfeasance, charges of which must be preferred in writing, by at least two members, to the congress in the case of a member of the judiciary department and to the judiciary department in the case of a member of another department.

### Precept Number 9

That in the event of vacancies or absences of members of the judiciary or the commissions for any cause, the remaining members of the judiciary or the commissions may temporarily fill the vacancies from the members of the previous congress to serve until the next congress convenes and elects their permanent successors.

### Precept Number 10

That the judiciary shall organize as a court, hear arguments and adjudicate all international disputes, and cause transcripts of its decisions to be transmitted to the secretary of the tribunal; shall convene for such portions of four months or longer as may be necessary to clear the docket in two sessions each year; and shall appoint a marshal and such assistants as may be necessary to bring before it those impeached, and otherwise maintain order. Members from the countries involved in disputes shall not sit on such cases.

### Precept Number 11

That the civil commission shall have control of and direct the organization and administration of the civil affairs of the tribunal.

### Precept Number 12

That the armament commission shall have control of and direct the organization and administration of the armament affairs of the tribunal, shall organize two general staffs of at least nine members each, no two of whom are to be from one nation, for directing land and sea operations, respectively, and whose acts shall be governed by majority rules; shall prescribe rules for the conduct of the armament forces; shall provide that commissioned and non-commissioned officers, troops, sailors, marines, mechanics, and others shall be drawn from the nations' present organizations and be amalgamated into one; that the armament forces shall be approximately 10% of those of the nations as they exist on a peace basis; and that the tribunal's forces shall be stationed in such numbers in different parts of the world at such times and of such nationalities as will enable the tribunal to enforce its decisions, suppress hostilities, and maintain the peace between nations.

### PRECEPT NUMBER 13

That a majority of the respective commissions shall govern and control the affairs thereof; that the duty of each chairman shall be to preside and promulgate the majority rulings to those in interest; that upon the call of a member of either of the commissions they shall meet in joint session to discuss and give consideration to matters of joint interest; that in event there is need to resort to arms against any nation, the civil and armament commissioners shall sit together and the chairman of the civil commission shall preside as chairman of the joint sessions; that a majority of the two commissions shall govern in determining the method of procedure; and that no member of a commission from a country against which armed forces are to be used shall sit at such joint sessions.

### PRECEPT NUMBER 14

That the two commissions shall prepare budgets for their respective needs for each succeeding year; that the civil commission shall prepare the budgets for the judiciary and the congress; and that these budgets shall be presented to the congress for its act of appropriation.

### PRECEPT NUMBER 15

That the secretary shall keep a record of the proceedings of the congress, transmit the same to the judiciary and the respective commissions interested, receive complaints from nations and transmit them to the judiciary, and transmit decisions of the judiciary to the nations interested and to the commissions for enforcement if necessary; and shall make a report thereon to the congress annually.

### Precept Number 16

That the treasurer shall receive and have the custody of the funds and investments of the tribunal and shall disburse the funds only upon warrants drawn by the comptroller against appropriations made by the congress.

### Precept Number 17

That the comptroller shall prescribe the system for and keep the accounts of the tribunal, and draw warrants on the treasurer for the disbursement of moneys on accounts stated which shall be approved by the respective chairmen of the two commissions, the chairman of the civil commission approving the accounts for the congress and the judiciary in accordance with appropriations made therefor; and shall make a report of the accounting and statistical affairs to the congress annually.

### Precept Number 18

That the expenditures of the tribunal shall not exceed 50% of the receipts from the nations in any one year; that the surplus of not less than 50% of the receipts shall be invested in the bonds of the countries contributing to the support of the tribunal, and the interest received from the bonds also shall be invested in bonds of such nations semiannually or as often as possible; that these investments shall be kept separate and be continued until the principal sum will yield in interest annually a sum 90% of which will suffice to support the tribunal, whereupon the nations may cease to make appropriations and payments in support of the tribunal; that thereafter the tribunal may expend 90% of the interest proceeds for its support and invest 10% which shall be kept separate and be accumulated for the general purposes of the tribunal.

### Precept Number 19

That the armament commission shall be empowered to dispose of the unnecessary ships, equipment, heavy ordnance, and other things incident thereto, and order the proceeds therefrom paid over to the treasurer to be added to the surplus of the tribunal and invested in national bonds.

These precepts are accompanied by a schedule showing the names of practically all the nations of the world, arranged alphabetically, their approximate population, the approximate number of officers and men in the armies and navies, and the cost per annum on a peace basis tabulated from the best obtainable sources, also the estimated size of the army of each nation, and the number of representatives to the congress of the tribunal according to this plan. The cost per annum is based on a five years' average for the larger nations. The schedule is divided into two groups, the countries marked with the letter (A) being the 20 largest, many with navies of formidable size.

On the world population of 1,624,000,000 there will be 75 representatives divided among 58 nations.

The plan provides that the members of the several departments are to be from different nations, thus making them thoroughly representative, for rotation of the members in office, and for the control of the commissions by the majorities thereof to prevent the possibility of the creation of a centralized individual power.

Considering the enormous powers with which the tribunal would be endowed under this plan, each participating nation should—and in all probability would—most carefully select its representative or representatives. These should be citizens of the highest repute, probity, distinction, and attainments, and it would follow that the tribunal and its component parts would thus comprise the very best types from all the nations.

While all nations should be parties to the precepts, it is doubtful if it would be expedient to include every nation in an estimate of appropriation and payment to the tribunal, for the reason that some of the smaller nations with little or no navies and with comparatively small armaments may need their present armies for internal protection. To make a conservative presentation of the cost of the tribunal as compared with the present cost to the nations, the expenditures of 20 foremost nations are used. The expenditures of these 20 nations for armaments represent about 95% of the total, and the men in their armies and navies represent about 85% of the total of all men so engaged.

The total expenditures for the armies and navies of the 20 nations on a peace basis amount to $2,405,000,000, divided $1,568,000,000 for the armies and $837,000,000 for the navies. The appropriations and payments to the peace tribunal under the proposed plan would be one-third of this amount, $522,000,000 for the armies and $279,000,000 for the navies, or a total of $801,000,000. It is estimated that these 20 nations would expend for their armies 50% of their present expenditures, or $784,000,000, and 10% of present expenditures for navies on account of the retired list which with incidentals would amount to $84,000,000, or a total of $868,000,000. This would make the total expenditures for these 20 nations $1,669,000,000, as compared with expenditures of $2,405,000,000 on a peace basis, resulting in an immediate and direct saving of $736,000,000 per annum, which will be increased as the retired list decreases and to which after 25 years will be added the annual amount that in the meantime will be paid to the tribunal, as after that time further payments to the tribunal will not be necessary, making a direct saving after the 25-year period of $1,537,000,000 per annum for the 20 nations in the group. In addition to this immediate and direct saving which would naturally go to increase the wealth of the various nations, the indirect savings would be incalculable but would none the less visibly affect every nation of the world.

On this basis, the peace tribunal would have available $801,000,000 per annum, one-half of which, or $400,500,000, invested and compounded annually for 25 years at 3%, would produce about $15,000,000,-000, 3% of which, or $450,000,000, would be the approximate annual income. Ninety per cent, or $405, 000,000, would be more than sufficient to maintain the peace tribunal thereafter without any expense to the nations and leave annually over $45,000,000 to be invested and compounded as a reserve fund. The other half, $400,500,000, would be available for the use of the tribunal which would require annually, approximately, for its civil organization $5,000,000, and for its armaments $395,500,000.

The expenditures for the congress, the judiciary, and the commissions of $5,000,000 include, roughly estimated, 75 representatives to the congress at $10,-000 each, $750,000, and mileage and contingencies $250,000, or, $1,000,000; nine members of the judiciary, nine civil commissioners, and nine armament commissioners, 27 in all, at $25,000 each, $675,000, and contingencies $325,000, or $1,000,000; a civil staff of deputies, chiefs, clerks, translators, marshals, messengers, and others, say 900, at salaries ranging from the deputies at $7,500, and scaling down for chiefs of bureaus, clerks, translators, and others, to the messengers at $500 each, an aggregate of $1,500,000, with contingencies $500,000, making a total of $2,000,000; and allowances for rent of offices and other contingencies of another $1,000,000.

The estimate of the armament, $395,500,000, covers the land forces of approximately 650,000 at an average cost per annum of $500 each, $325,000,000; men, maintenance, and operation of ships at a trifle less than 10% of the aggregate of all the navies of the world, $70,000,000, and incidental office expenses of the general staffs, $500,000.

The land forces as provided by these precepts should be divided so that they would be stationed in various parts of the world approximately as follows:

| | |
|---|---|
| Western Europe | 100,000 |
| Central Europe | 100,000 |
| Southeastern Europe | 50,000 |
| Northern Africa | 50,000 |
| Southern Africa | 50,000 |
| Northern India | 50,000 |
| Eastern China | 50,000 |
| North America | 100,000 |
| South America | 100,000 |

It should be provided further by the general staff that not more than approximately 25% of the forces stationed in the territory of any nation may be natives of that particular nation. All of these forces

## Approximate Population, Men and Cost per Year of Armies and Navies on Peace Basis of Practically All Nations, and Estimated Number of Men in Armies and Number of Representatives Under Proposed Plan of a World's Peace Tribunal

| Nations (Including Dependencies) | Population | Armies—Peace Basis | | Navies—Peace Basis | | Total Armies and Navies | | On Basis of Proposed Plan | |
|---|---|---|---|---|---|---|---|---|---|
| | | Number of Men | Cost per Annum | Number of Men | Cost per Annum | Number of Men | Cost per Annum | Number of Men, Armies | Number of Representatives |
| Abyssinia | 8,000,000 | 150,000 | * $1,000,000 | ..... | .......... | 150,000 | $1,000,000 | 4,000 | 1 |
| Afghanistan | 6,000,000 | 55,000 | * 1,000,000 | ..... | .......... | 55,000 | 1,000,000 | 3,000 | 1 |
| Albania | 850,000 | * 7,000 | * 2,000,000 | ..... | .......... | 7,000 | 2,000,000 | 1,000 | 1 |
| Andorra | 5,000 | ...... | .......... | ..... | .......... | ...... | .......... | ..... | 1 |
| Arabia, Central (Nedjed et al) | 1,000,000 | ...... | .......... | ..... | .......... | ...... | .......... | ..... | 1 |
| Argentine (A) | 7,500,000 | 23,000 | 18,000,000 | 6,000 | * $7,000,000 | 29,000 | 25,000,000 | 4,000 | 1 |
| Austria-Hungary (A) | 50,000,000 | 413,000 | 108,000,000 | 23,000 | 29,000,000 | 436,000 | 137,000,000 | 25,000 | 2 |
| Belgium (A) | 23,000,000 | 70,000 | 20,000,000 | ..... | .......... | 70,000 | 20,000,000 | 11,000 | 1 |
| Bhutan | 250,000 | ...... | .......... | ..... | .......... | ...... | .......... | ..... | 1 |
| Bolivia (A) | 2,000,000 | 3,000 | 2,000,000 | ..... | .......... | 3,000 | 2,000,000 | 1,000 | 1 |
| Brazil (A) | 24,000,000 | 23,000 | 25,000,000 | 8,000 | 16,000,000 | 31,000 | 41,000,000 | 12,000 | 1 |
| Bulgaria (A) | 4,500,000 | 60,000 | 8,000,000 | * 1,000 | * 1,000,000 | 61,000 | 9,000,000 | 2,000 | 1 |
| Chile (A) | 3,500,000 | 22,000 | 9,000,000 | 7,000 | 7,000,000 | 29,000 | 16,000,000 | 2,000 | 1 |
| China (A) | 320,000,000 | 237,000 | † 25,000,000 | * 1,000 | † 2,000,000 | 238,000 | 27,000,000 | 175,000 | 4 |
| Colombia | 5,400,000 | 6,000 | * 2,000,000 | 1,000 | * 1,000,000 | 7,000 | 3,000,000 | 3,000 | 1 |
| Costa Rica | 400,000 | 1,000 | .......... | ..... | .......... | 1,000 | .......... | 1,000 | 1 |
| Cuba | 2,500,000 | 12,000 | * 3,000,000 | 1,000 | * 1,000,000 | 13,000 | 4,000,000 | 1,000 | 1 |
| Denmark (A) | 3,000,000 | 14,000 | 5,000,000 | 4,000 | 3,000,000 | 18,000 | 8,000,000 | 2,000 | 1 |
| Equador | 1,500,000 | 8,000 | * 2,000,000 | ..... | .......... | 8,000 | 2,000,000 | 1,000 | 1 |
| France (A) | 82,000,000 | 759,000 | 223,000,000 | 37,000 | 87,000,000 | 796,000 | 310,000,000 | 41,000 | 2 |
| Germany (A) | 77,000,000 | 817,000 | 222,000,000 | 71,000 | 116,000,000 | 888,000 | 338,000,000 | 38,000 | 2 |
| Great Britain (A) | 424,000,000 | 460,000 | 249,000,000 | 133,000 | 240,000,000 | 593,000 | 489,000,000 | 212,000 | 4 |
| Greece | 4,500,000 | 25,000 | 4,000,000 | 4,000 | 4,000,000 | 29,000 | 8,000,000 | 2,000 | 1 |
| Guatemala | 2,000,000 | 6,000 | 6,000,000 | * 1,000 | * 1,000,000 | 7,000 | 7,000,000 | 1,000 | 1 |
| Haiti | 2,500,000 | 6,000 | * 1,000,000 | ..... | .......... | 6,000 | 1,000,000 | 1,000 | 1 |
| Honduras | 500,000 | 31,000 | * 1,000,000 | ..... | .......... | 31,000 | 1,000,000 | 1,000 | 1 |
| Italy (A) | 36,000,000 | 323,000 | 79,000,000 | 38,000 | 41,000,000 | 361,000 | 120,000,000 | 18,000 | 2 |
| Japan (A) | 67,000,000 | 250,000 | 50,000,000 | 51,000 | 47,000,000 | 301,000 | 97,000,000 | 33,000 | 2 |

| | | | | | | | | | |
|---|---|---|---|---|---|---|---|---|---|
| Liberia | 2,000,000 | ...... | ........... | ..... | .......... | ...... | ........... | ..... | 1 |
| Liechtenstein | 10,000 | ...... | ........... | ..... | .......... | ...... | ........... | ..... | 1 |
| Luxemburg | 250,000 | ...... | ........... | ..... | .......... | ...... | ........... | ..... | 1 |
| Mexico | 15,500,000 | 30,000 | 11,000,000 | 1,000 | * 2,000,000 | 31,000 | 13,000,000 | 7,500 | 1 |
| Monaco | 23,000 | ...... | ........... | ..... | .......... | ...... | ........... | ..... | 1 |
| Montenegro | 500,000 | * 4,000 | 1,000,000 | ..... | .......... | 4,000 | 1,000,000 | 1,000 | 1 |
| Morocco | 5,000,000 | ...... | ........... | ..... | .......... | ...... | ........... | ..... | 1 |
| Nepal | 5,000,000 | 30,000 | ........... | ..... | .......... | 30,000 | ........... | 2,500 | 1 |
| Netherlands (A) | 44,000,000 | 71,000 | 30,000,000 | 11,000 | 8,000,000 | 82,000 | 38,000,000 | 22,000 | 2 |
| Nicaragua | 600,000 | 3,000 | ........... | ..... | .......... | 3,000 | ........... | 1,000 | 1 |
| Norway | 2,500,000 | 35,000 | 4,000,000 | 1,000 | * 1,000,000 | 36,000 | 5,000,000 | 1,000 | 1 |
| Oman | 500,000 | ...... | ........... | ..... | .......... | ...... | ........... | ..... | 1 |
| Panama | 427,000 | * 3,000 | * 1,000,000 | ..... | .......... | 3,000 | 1,000,000 | 1,000 | 1 |
| Paraguay | 800,000 | 3,000 | * 1,000,000 | ..... | .......... | 3,000 | 1,000,000 | 1,000 | 1 |
| Persia | 9,500,000 | ...... | ........... | ..... | .......... | ...... | ........... | ..... | 1 |
| Peru | 4,500,000 | 65,000 | * 4,000,000 | ..... | .......... | 65,000 | 4,000,000 | 2,000 | 1 |
| Portugal | 15,000,000 | 33,000 | 11,000,000 | 6,000 | * 2,000,000 | 39,000 | 13,000,000 | 7,500 | 1 |
| Roumania | 7,000,000 | 101,000 | 14,000,000 | * 2,000 | * 2,000,000 | 103,000 | 16,000,000 | 4,000 | 1 |
| Russia (A) | 171,000,000 | 1,230,000 | 318,000,000 | 53,000 | 75,000,000 | 1,283,000 | 393,000,000 | 85,000 | 3 |
| Salvador | 1,500,000 | 16,000 | ........... | ..... | .......... | 16,000 | ........... | 1,000 | 1 |
| Santo Domingo | 600,000 | 1,000 | ........... | ..... | .......... | 1,000 | ........... | 1,000 | 1 |
| Servia | 4,500,000 | 361,000 | 1,000,000 | ..... | .......... | 361,000 | 1,000,000 | 3,000 | 1 |
| Siam | 8,000,000 | 20,000 | * 3,000,000 | 10,000 | * 4,000,000 | 30,000 | 7,000,000 | 4,000 | 1 |
| Spain (A) | 19,500,000 | 123,000 | 35,000,000 | 9,000 | 13,000,000 | 132,000 | 48,000,000 | 10,000 | 1 |
| Sweden | 5,500,000 | 80,000 | 14,000,000 | 6,000 | * 3,000,000 | 86,000 | 17,000,000 | 3,000 | 1 |
| Switzerland (A) | 3,500,000 | 35,000 | 9,000,000 | ..... | .......... | 35,000 | 9,000,000 | 2,000 | 1 |
| Turkey (A) | 32,500,000 | 247,000 | 30,000,000 | 37,000 | 6,000,000 | 284,000 | 36,000,000 | 16,000 | 2 |
| United States (A) | 102,000,000 | 85,000 | 103,000,000 | 60,000 | 139,000,000 | 145,000 | 242,000,000 | 51,000 | 3 |
| Uruguay | 1,000,000 | 10,000 | * 3,000,000 | ..... | .......... | 10,000 | 3,000,000 | 1,000 | 1 |
| Venezuela | 2,500,000 | 10,000 | * 3,000,000 | ..... | .......... | 10,000 | 3,000,000 | 1,000 | 1 |
| Totals—All Nations | 1,624,115,000 | 6,377,000 | $1,662,000,000 | 583,000 | $858,000,000 | 6,960,000 | $2,520,000,000 | 823,500 | 75 |
| Totals of Nations marked (A), being the 20 largest, many with formidable navies | 1,496,000,000 | 5,265,000 | $1,568,000,000 | 550,000 | $837,000,000 | 5,815,000 | $2,405,000,000 | 762,000 | |

* Arbitrarily estimated for the totals mostly from other figures in this exhibit.
† Arbitrarily estimated for the totals used for the armies and navies.

would be moved from time to time and from place to place to meet the exigencies of the tribunal.

The sea forces would be similarly divided between the waters of the principal nations and similarly moved about to meet the exigencies of the tribunal.

The number of men in the armies and navies of the nations of the world, on a peace basis, is approximately 6,960,000. It is estimated that for the armament of the peace tribunal there would be required 700,000 men—land forces 650,000, sea forces 50,000—and for the standing armies of the nations and retired lists less than 900,000 men, making available over 5,000,000 disciplined men whose occupation in peaceful pursuits would add materially to the world's economic value.

All of the approximations and estimates have been prepared with care and are believed to be conservative, but they are intended to be illustrative and illuminative only.

If the causes of modern wars be analyzed and considered in connection with the proposed plan, it is apparent that under every condition a tribunal such as is proposed would have had control of the situation and would have prevented hostilities between the nations.

Editorial Note: The Hague Tribunal, having been established in 1899, was already a number of years old when the Great War, with all its fury, burst forth upon the world. The natural question has been frequently asked, when various other proposals insuring peace have since been made, concerning why the Permanent Court of Arbitration, as the Hague Tribunal was known, did not afford the opportunity and machinery for settling the differences out of which the Great War arose and for preventing that gigantic struggle.

The Hague Tribunal was a sort of "come in and talk it over" affair. It was not empowered to adjudicate disputes or enforce ideas as to settlement. Its function was arbitral rather than judicial, and the Tribunal would have been impotent, therefore, to force a settlement of the controversy underlying the Great War, unless the parties thereto had agreed to the recommendations of the court.

The Covenant of the League of Nations provides for an assembly of delegates, an executive council, a permanent secretariat, and the establishment of a permanent court of international justice. The League is therefore clothed with judicial rather than arbitral authority, and the court established under the covenant differs in that respect from the Hague Tribunal.

But, again, the League is empowered only by implication to enforce any findings. This implication is found in Article 11, which reserves to the high contracting parties "the right to take any action which may be deemed wise and effectual to safeguard the peace of nations." Former President Wilson may have intended to so interpret this provision, when, in presenting the report of the commission which considered and drafted the Covenant of the League of Nations, he is reported as having said: "Armed force is in the background of this program, but it is in the background, and if the moral force of the world will not suffice, the physical force of the world shall. But that is the last resort, because this is intended as a constitution of peace, not as a league of war."

Mr. Sells, whose plan of international peace was offered before any public suggestion of a League of Nations had been made, comes out courageously and without reservation in favor of a tribunal not only with authority to adjudicate, but with power, in the form of a world army and navy, to enforce its findings. Nothing is left to implication, and there is no doubt in this respect as to what the scheme contemplates.

The commissions suggested by Mr. Sells appear to offer a way much more simple and less cumbersome for administering the plan than the assembly, executive council, secretariat, and court provided by the League. His plan may be characterized as more of a business plan than a legal one. It is concise, filled with ideas rather than verbiage, and takes into consideration a very important factor in any plan, namely, the manner in which it is to be financed and the economy which it would effect, as well as the other advantages which would accrue. Obviously, estimates made in 1915 would now have to be revised in the light of present conditions.

The League of Nations, in so far as may be ascertained from public information, appears to have disregarded the cost of operation, except as provision is made for the apportionment of expenses of the secretariat among states members of the League on the basis of the expense distribution used by the International Bureau of the Universal Postal Union. The makers of the covenant proceeded apparently on the theory that if the purposes of the League were justifiable the expense of operating it would be a matter of secondary consideration. It strikes one as being essentially a political program rather than anything else, and appears not to have given due regard to the economic relations existing among nations.

While Mr. Sells has not particularly stressed this point it seems probable that working under the influence of an agreement such as he has proposed the inclinations of those entrusted with the administration would be to give a large measure of consideration to the economic aspect of affairs among nations. This would, perhaps, go as far in the direction of preventing wars as any scheme which might be worked out.

International jealousies growing out of various trade relations and business aspirations may possibly have constituted the motives for past wars to an extent greater than is usually believed. It seems doubtful, therefore, that any scheme will succeed which does not take this matter into consideration, and, further, one of the important results must be, as Mr. Sells points out, some measure of national economy accruing to the states members at interest.

The satisfactory settlement of the permanent peace question appears to be almost as far away as ever, and it seems not unreasonable to venture the opinion that before a workable scheme is reached, consideration will have to be given to some of the outstanding principles embodied in Mr. Sells' plan.

# XIV

# PROPOSED PLAN FOR HANDLING INTERLINE FREIGHT CLAIMS

# XIV

# PROPOSED PLAN FOR HANDLING INTERLINE FREIGHT CLAIMS

Presentation. Exhibit A: Outline of proposed plan for handling interline freight claims. Exhibit B: Outline of present methods. Exhibit C: Briefs of certain claims. Exhibit D: Statistics relating to claims. Exhibit E: Claims involving amounts in various classifications. Exhibit F: Names of carriers in the southeastern territory and approximate mileage.

Editorial Note: Importance of report. Adoption of plan by practically all railroads in the United States. This engagement is characteristic of many which Mr. Sells directed involving a public interest.

---

HASKINS & SELLS
CERTIFIED PUBLIC ACCOUNTANTS
30 BROAD STREET
NEW YORK

LONDON, E C
30 COLEMAN STREET

CABLE ADDRESS HASKSELLS

CHICAGO 204 DEARBORN STREET | ST. LOUIS LINCOLN TRUST BUILDING | CLEVELAND WILLIAMSON BUILDING | PITTSBURG FARMERS BANK BUILDING

New York, December 31, 1904

R. G. Erwin, Esq.,
President, Atlantic Coast Line Railroad Company, New York

Samuel Spencer, Esq.,
President, Southern Railway Company, New York

J. C. Welling, Esq.,
Vice-President, Illinois Central Railroad Company, Chicago

J. M. Barr, Esq.,
President, Seaboard Air Line Railway, Portsmouth

Geo. W. Stevens, Esq.,
President, Chesapeake & Ohio Railway Company, Richmond

Committee appointed at a meeting of the presidents of the railways in the southeastern territory, held in New York, October 28, 1904, to consider and recommend a method for the prompt settlement of interline claims with claimants and the prompt adjustment of the same as between the carriers in interest.

GENTLEMEN:

In accordance with your request, an examination has been made of the present methods of handling interline freight claims in the offices of nearly all the lines represented at the meeting of presidents held in New York, October 28, 1904, together with a study of the causes which have occasioned the present unsatisfactory conditions, with a view to submitting for your consideration, and for your recommendation to the presidents of the carriers in interest, a plan for the prompt settlement of interline claims with claimants and the prompt adjustment of the same as between the carriers.

It is well known that much time is consumed in the adjustment and final settlement of interline claims, and it is generally conceded by all who have knowledge of the business that they are handled in a cumbersome way, inflicting injustice upon claimants to such an extent that state laws, adverse to carriers in respect to freight claims, have been already passed in some of the southeastern states, and are threatened in other states; also that the carriers suffer great delays in making settlements between themselves, and are subject to heavy expense in conducting interline claim work.

Several of the carriers in the southeastern territory receive as many as 500 new claims in a day; in some cases more; and in the case of one of the carriers there are received about 1,000 claims a day. The claims filed are continually increasing both in number and amount, and in far greater ratio than is warranted by the increase in freight earnings; and this disproportion is being augmented year by year.

The intricacies now involved in investigating many of the interline claims are numerous and extensive, multiplying the complications necessary to be considered before disposition of the case can be made.

It is estimated that more than 70% of the new claims filed in the southeastern territory are interline claims; that 75% of these interline claims are wholly settled by the carriers within the southeastern territory; that interline claims involve an average of three carriers; that it takes from two to three times as much work to settle an interline claim as to settle a local claim, and from two to ten times as long a period of time; and that an average of only about two-thirds of the interline claims against all the carriers in the southeastern territory are disposed of within six months from the time they are filed, the remaining one-third consuming a much longer time. Many of the claims are in process of investigation for two or three years, and some of them drag on still longer.

Among the causes for these delays may be mentioned the following:

(*a*) The cumbersome practice of sending all the claim papers to all the carriers interested; first to one carrier, then to another carrier, and so on, and finally back, usually through the same channel, to the carrier with which the claim originated; and that not once only, but in many cases several times.

(*b*) A general evading of responsibility for participation in claims, together with inefficient handling. Sometimes the most trivial excuses are offered as objections, and not infrequently these excuses are wholly groundless and not to the point. In many cases all original claim papers are lost, necessitating laborious attempts at duplication.

(*c*) The unbusiness-like principle involved in one carrier's having to obtain another carrier's permission to make a distribution and charge already determined through the investigation.

Contributory to these causes may also be mentioned imperfect records and reports of "over, short, and damage" and of "exceptions" made at terminal, junction, and transfer points; incomplete files of rates and divisions; and insufficient interline billing.

The interests of the carriers in interline claims are mutual in all respects; the action of one is the concern of all; the settling carrier is but the agent.

Some of the prerequisites to enabling the carriers to overcome the present objectionable conditions successfully, and to handle interline claims with reasonable dispatch, must embrace, with others, the following radical changes:

(*a*) There should be absolute good faith between the carriers, such as now exists in the interline freight and interline ticket settlements.

(*b*) There must be an immediate investigation of each interline claim simultaneously, locally, and among all the carriers in interest, without sending the original papers out of the office of the carrier settling the claim. The investigation between the carriers should be merely for the purpose of establishing the condition—what might be called the physical condition of the claim—and should not involve the question of the distribution.

(*c*) When the investigation has been made, and the claimant settled with, the distribution between the carriers of the amount of the claim should be made by the carrier making the settlement with the claimant.

There is submitted herewith an outline of a proposed plan for handling interline claims, marked Exhibit "A," together with five additional exhibits, marked "B" to "F," and comments thereon, as follows:

EXHIBITS

"A" OUTLINE OF PROPOSED PLAN FOR HANDLING INTERLINE FREIGHT CLAIMS (Page 209).

"B" OUTLINE OF PRESENT METHODS OF SOME OF THE CARRIERS REPRESENTED AT THE MEETING HELD OCTOBER 28, 1904 (Page 213).

"C" BRIEFS OF CERTAIN CLAIMS REVIEWED IN THE OFFICES OF SOME OF THE CARRIERS, AND NOTES ON CLAIMS (Page 226).

"D" STATISTICS RELATING TO CLAIMS RECEIVED DURING THE YEAR ENDED JUNE 30, 1904, BY EIGHT OF THE CARRIERS (Page 248).

"E" CLAIMS INVOLVING AMOUNTS OF $1 AND UNDER, $2.50

AND UNDER, $5 AND UNDER, AND $10 AND UNDER (Page 251).

"F" NAMES OF CARRIERS IN THE SOUTHEASTERN TERRITORY AND APPROXIMATE MILEAGE AS SHOWN BY THE OFFICIAL GUIDE (Page 252).

COMMENTS (Page 258).

The plan proposed will accomplish the following results:

1. Prompt settlement of interline claims with claimants;

2. Prompt settlement of interline claims between carriers;

3. Discontinuance of transmission of voluminous claim papers back and forth between the carriers;

4. Facility for prompt adjustment, through an Arbitration Bureau, of differences when they arise between the carriers;

5. A saving estimated at about 50% of the present cost of handling interline claims. The saving will vary according to conditions existing in the various offices. In some cases where there may not be sufficient help at present, the reduction would not be so large. Whatever proportion of saving can be made should be partly realized by the end of the first year and fully realized by the end of the second year.

The plan should be made effective at some future date to be agreed upon; should be applicable to all claims filed on and after that date; but should not be retroactive.

Consideration has been given to a plan for absorbing all amounts paid by the respective carriers without making any adjustment between the carriers; also to a plan for the establishment of a clearing-house; and both plans have been rejected as impracticable. In the former, it is found that generally there is a great difference between the amount involved in the claims paid by any one carrier for account of the other carriers and the amount paid by the other carriers for account of that one carrier. In the latter, it is believed that, under present conditions, such an organization would be unwieldy because of its size, and therefore difficult, if not impossible, to operate efficiently.

The successful operation of the proposed plan would doubtless result in its adoption by other carriers, and, in a comparatively short time, in its general adoption throughout the country. The greater the number of carriers becoming parties to the plan, the better will it be for all concerned.

Yours truly,

E. W. SELLS, C. P. A.

## EXHIBIT "A"

### OUTLINE OF PROPOSED PLAN FOR HANDLING INTERLINE FREIGHT CLAIMS

Each interline claim, when filed, should be immediately investigated by the carrier to which presented, and should be settled by such carrier with the claimant upon its merits—paid, compromised, or declined—irrespective of the amount to be distributed against the other carriers in interest. So far as practicable, claims should be presented to and settled by the delivering carriers.

There should be retained in the office of the carrier making the settlement the necessary and usual claim papers, such as the bill of lading, freight bill, and other original papers.

Immediately upon the receipt of the claim, a brief, or "base," as it is usually called, should be made of the principal facts as shown by the bill of lading, the freight bill, and other original papers. This basis should be made on a form, or blank, specially prepared for the purpose, having in the upper part conveniently arranged spaces for filling in the principal facts, and in the lower part, space for the necessary inquiries and responses. Different forms may be used advantageously for overcharge and loss and damage cases. In order to facilitate the clerical work, there should be made at one writing, by the use of carbons, as many copies of the base as may be needed for the purpose of sending one to each of the carriers in interest and for the local investigation. These copies, containing such inquiry as is directly pertinent to the question involved, should be sent simultaneously to all the carriers in interest. The base must be handled promptly by these carriers and returned to the carrier making the inquiry, with such full reply as will afford to the settling carrier the greatest facility in dealing with the claimant. This will enable the settling carrier to have promptly, in connection with the original papers, all the facts which it has been possible to ascertain in regard to the condition of the claim.

The amount of each claim should be distributed by the carrier making the settlement, against the carrier or carriers interested in the claim: in a case of overcharge, where the overcharge occurs; in a case of loss or damage, where the responsibility for the loss or damage is located. When the investigation fails to locate the overcharge or the responsibility for the loss or damage, the amount of the claim should be distributed against the carriers in interest upon the basis of the revenue or the mileage, according to the rules of the Freight Claim Association. Claims for amounts under such amount as shall be fixed as the minimum should be absorbed by the delivering carrier and not distributed against the other carrier or carriers in interest.

A notice, showing the amount of the distribution, filled in on a suitable form prepared for the purpose, should be sent by the settling carrier to the respective carrier or carriers in interest, as soon as the distribution is made. Each carrier receiving such notice of distribution should send an acceptance to the carrier making the settlement; and such acceptance will be authority for a draft. In case an evidently erroneous notice of distribution is sent, it may be returned rejected, with the error clearly indicated. The acceptance or rejection should be made within 15 days.

Settlement between carriers should be made as frequently as once a month. The carrier sending the notice of distribution should also send a statement to each carrier, recapitulating the accepted notices sent during any given period, and within 30 days after the close of the period during which the notices have been sent, and should make drafts on the respective carriers for the amounts shown by the statements.

Upon the completion of the investigation, all the papers in each claim should be filed by the carrier making the settlement with the claimant, without being sent to the other carrier or carriers in interest, except as hereafter provided in the plan, and should be kept at least three years in files convenient for ready reference.

When a question shall arise as to the justice or propriety of a distribution made by the settling carrier, the objecting carrier may ask for the claim papers, or, if preferred, may have access to the files of interline claims in the settling carrier's office. The papers are not to be thus demanded or examined unless there is some apparent evidence of a wrong distribution, or of something unusual in the case, or unless a considerable amount is involved; the purpose of this caution being to avoid undue attention to trivial matters. When the papers are withdrawn from the files of the carrier making the settlement, they should be returned within 15 days. When more than one carrier has asked for the papers, they should be furnished in the order in which the requests are received.

There should be an Arbitration Bureau established by the carriers adopting this plan, organized for the purpose of settling questions that may arise between the carriers in interest respecting the distribution of interline claims.

When the carrier settling a claim is in doubt about the distribution to be made against the carrier or carriers in interest, the claim may be referred to the Arbitration Bureau, before the distribution against the carrier or carriers in interest is made, for a ruling; and such ruling shall be final.

When a question shall arise between the carriers in interest regarding a claim that has been paid and included in a statement upon which a settlement has been made, the objecting carrier may have the claim papers referred to the Arbitration Bureau for a ruling upon the distribution; and such ruling shall be final.

If an objecting carrier shall obtain a favorable decision from the Arbitrator on a claim referred, the amount involved should be distributed in accordance therewith and included in the next statement of settlement.

Any claim referred for arbitration should be sent to the Bureau within three months of the date of the statement of settlement in which included.

The expense of maintaining the Arbitration Bureau should be apportioned between the carriers in interest in the ratio of their published gross freight earnings. A working fund should be provided for the Arbitration Bureau.

A fee should be charged for arbitrating each claim; say of $5 each for claims of $50 or under, and $10 each for claims of over $50. The fee for the arbitration should be paid by the carrier against which the decision is made. A fee of, say, $2.50 for each claim should be charged against the carrier applying to the Arbitration Bureau for a ruling before distribution. The amounts so charged should, when collected, be deducted from the expense of the Bureau which is to be apportioned between the carriers.

When a claim involves a carrier or carriers not having adopted this plan, the carrier making the settlement will, of course, be obliged to proceed in the same cumbersome manner as at present with such carrier or carriers; but this need not interfere with the method of procedure in the local investigation, nor in that with the carrier or carriers adopting this plan.

## EXHIBIT "B"

### OUTLINE OF PRESENT METHODS OF SOME OF THE CARRIERS REPRESENTED AT THE MEETING HELD OCTOBER 28, 1904, AS REPORTED BY THEM RESPECTIVELY

### ATLANTIC COAST LINE RAILROAD COMPANY

When a new claim reaches this office it goes first to the Claim Entry Desk, where a proper record of the claim is made in the Claim Entry book and the claim given a number. It is then passed to the Overcharge or Loss and Damage investigators, according to the nature of the claim. The investigator stamps his individual number on it so as to insure rehandling it when returned to this office.

All claims local to his company are charged off to Loss and Damage Account in cases of claims of loss and damage, or are charged to Freight Earnings in cases of overcharge. When said claims are ready to be paid the investigator attaches a form slip to papers, authorizing the payment and showing whether the entire amount is to be charged to the Atlantic Coast Line or charged back to the freight claim agent when connecting lines are involved. The papers are sent to the Atlantic Coast Line agent at point where claim was filed, who, after payment, lists the claim with the auditor of freight receipts for his credit, and the auditor of freight receipts then charges the amount in accordance with the form attached by us, above referred to.

Regarding claims filed against foreign lines, in which we are interested: as soon as our liability is discovered, we attach to papers a draft authority for the proper amount, which accompanies papers back to the original line, which detaches the draft authority and collects through the auditing department. We make a carbon copy of every endorsement we attach to a claim, which carbon copy is filed with what we term our "base file" relating to the claim in question.

## Chicago and Eastern Illinois Railroad Company

We have but two (2) forms for the presentation of claims through our agents.

Form 424 is a blank for transmission of claim by agents to this office and is convenient, as it not only provides spaces for way-bill reference and full particulars of billing, but also gives instructions on the back thereof, which, if complied with, avoids return of papers to the agent, which was almost invariably necessary before this blank was adopted.

Form 423 is for agent's relief, and instructions contained thereon are self-explanatory.

It is our practice to immediately voucher claims for overcharge in rate properly supported, when billing has been verified by the auditor and provided also that rate claimed is based on published tariff. If a foreign line is interested, the amount is carried in suspense until such time as proper authority is secured to debit the line or lines involved, when the auditor is requested to relieve Suspense Account and collect according to authorities obtained. Overcharges in weight or claims arising by reason of erroneous routing or other complication, are taken up with connecting lines and fully investigated before voucher is drawn.

Loss and damage claims, if the liability of the carriers is fully established when presented, are also immediately vouchered and if a foreign line is interested, carried in suspense until proper authority of connections is secured. Original freight bills of foreign lines frequently show exceptions as to condition or check of the property at time of delivery in the handwriting of agent or party making out freight bill, and this, by us, is considered *prima facie* evidence that the carriers are responsible for the loss or damage. Such claims are adjusted immediately, as well as claims in which we are the delivering line and already have report on file showing check or condition at time of delivery.

The proportion of our loss and damage claims adjusted prior to investigation, with us is necessarily limited as we have so many claims presented here by shippers on consignments destined to points on foreign lines, far removed, which require the handling of papers through each connection in order to follow up billing reference at each junction point and finally locate record at time of delivery. The universal adoption of through billing would eradicate many of our troubles on claims of this character as we would often be in a position to determine our liability, to the claimant, by one reference of papers to agent at destination, whereas under our present system, we must wait several months and sometimes a year or more before adjustment can be made, particularly if there are several lines in interest. Through billing would also eliminate entirely many claims which arise now from errors that occur at transfer points in rebilling the consignee's name and address, car number, initials or other particulars that must be given correctly to the delivery agent and result in loss or overcharge to the owner.

Vouchers for loss and damage, grain-doors, car-service and storage are referred to the general superintendent for approval. Vouchers for overcharge on coal are all referred to the coal traffic manager. Vouchers for all other overcharge claims go to the general freight department for approval, as well as claims for switching, drayage, milling in transit, and so on. As soon as the voucher has been approved by the proper department in accordance with the above, it is returned with all papers to the freight claim department, where the voucher is copied and duly numbered and referred, in turn, to the auditor who certifies that same has been examined and found correct; also that it has been duly registered in the auditor's office. The voucher is then approved for payment by the vice-president and returned to the auditor's office, the papers being filed with the voucher stub in the audit department and the voucher sent to the cashier for necessary record and payment. When a foreign road is interested, papers are forwarded with bill.

### Georgia Railroad

When a claim is presented to an agent of the Georgia Railroad, the agent attaches the necessary papers and forwards same to the general freight agent's office. The claim is then entered on the claim register, a brief taken, and the papers are referred to the auditor, who checks the billing and records the claim number on his office copy of the way-bill. The papers are returned by the auditor to the general freight agent's office with information as to the correctness of the copy of billing accompanying the claim, and whether any previous claim number is recorded against that particular way-bill. If the claim is one for overcharge it is then verified, and if correct is vouchered. If the Georgia Railroad alone is interested the voucher will show that the entire amount of the overcharge is to be charged to the Georgia Railroad and the claim is sent to the agent to whom it was presented, for payment. When paid he forwards the papers for relief to the auditor, who gives him the necessary credit and charges the amount of the claim to the proper account. If other lines are involved, the distribution of the overcharge is shown on the voucher, and the papers take the same course as above described, up to the point where the claim is received by the auditor. He charges the claim to the General Freight Agent's Suspense Account after giving the agent the necessary credit, and the claim is then handled by the general freight agent with other lines interested, and when authority is obtained from connections for their proportions, the claim is charged back to the auditor, on a form accompanied by a slip showing distribution of the amount of the various lines as shown by their "Claim Authority Form" similar to one used by the Georgia Railroad.

The same plan of settlement is pursued in the case of loss and damage claims.

### Louisville & Nashville Railroad Company

We divide our new claims, when received, into different series, indicating whether they are north- or south-bound overcharge, whether loss or damage, whether filed direct against the Louisville & Nashville or received through connections, whether paid claims or whether for relief of agents. These series are indicated by letters. When claim papers reach the office they are given a number and registered, and referred to the auditor for billing and check against his audited records; when the papers are returned the claim is ready for investigation. If the claim is for overcharge, and the shipment is one which has moved between points on the Louisville & Nashville Road, we check the claim in all particulars, and if it is found to be correct, voucher is prepared at once and payment is made through our agent located at the point at which the claim was filed, or through the treasurer's office, whichever is most convenient.

If the claim is one in which a connecting line is interested it is necessary to ascertain the basis of settlement at the junction point, through the office of the agent at the junction point, as well as the auditor's office. When returned with information as to settlement with connecting line, statement is made up showing the correct through rate and divisions which should have been applied and the amount of overcharge due by each line. The papers are then sent to the freight claim agent or other proper representative of connecting line for authority to adjust.

Overcharge claims filed against connections and sent to us for investigation are also sent to the auditor for check and verification of junction settlement. When returned by the auditor with advice as to the basis of settlement at the junction, the rates and divisions are verified and if found that we have overcharged, connecting lines are authorized to charge us with the proportion due from this company.

Where the Louisville & Nashville is an intermediate line in the handling of any freight, claims for overcharge are sent to the other interested lines for investigation by them before authority is given by the Louisville & Nashville for settlement; as soon as such connections return papers with proper authority, we verify the rates and divisions, attaching authority to cover the proportion due by the Louisville & Nashville and return papers to the connection from which originally received.

Loss and damage claims received from connecting lines, as well as our own loss and damage claims, are handled in the same way, for the reason it is necessary to obtain the billing from the agent before being sent to the auditor's office for his check and verification of the record, and endorsement made thereon to the effect that claim has been presented, in order to prevent duplication; and, in addition, it is necessary to make investigation through the division superintendents and others to ascertain whether or not the amount of the claim, or any part of it, is due by the Louisville & Nashville Railroad.

In handling loss and damage claims for $10 and less, they

are now settled by most of the lines south of the Ohio River without investigation to locate responsibility. Of course, proper distribution is made later. We have occasion to send such claims to the agent or division office in order to call attention to the manner in which the shipment was handled. That is to say, claims for the amount named, or less, are settled without delay and the adjustment of same is made later; but the same amount of work is performed on claims of this character that is performed on claims for larger amounts.

### Nashville, Chattanooga & St. Louis Railway Company

In our method of handling claims they are divided into three classes; namely, those filed with us by claimant, which we term "Local," those received from other carriers, termed "Foreign," and those paid through agents and remitted as "Cash," termed "Suspense." Each of the three classes of claims is recorded and handled under a separate series of numbers.

On receipt of the claims they are classified as above, recorded, numbered, and checked against the auditor's record of billing, when they are apportioned among the investigators for attention, the assignment of work to the individual being effected with a view of making each investigator a specialist on certain classes of claims. For instance, one investigator handles all north-bound lumber claims; another, south-bound C D & F, and so on.

In addition to the book record showing name of claimant, amount and nature of claim, we keep a file consisting of copies of all communications, billing, and so forth, on the base, arranged numerically in standard file boxes.

The investigator handles each claim as circumstances may require. Overcharge claims presented against this line, if found correct, are vouchered at once, and if other carriers are interested the proportion which may be due from them is charged to "Suspense" to be collected after settlement has been made with claimants. Legitimate loss and damage claims are also vouchered, with divisions in "Suspense," where the circumstances warrant such action, though the great majority of such claims are investigated by all lines in interest before payment is made.

Any claims received from other carriers are given immediate attention with view of authorizing drafts against this company for such amount as may be due under the rules and facts or passed on to the next line in interest.

"Suspense" claims—those paid by local agents on presentation—are inspected, and when the loss and damage or overcharge, as the case may be, is located with this company they are charged off to the proper account. When it appears that other carriers are interested the papers are submitted to them for authority, and so forth.

Under agreement with certain of our connections, we may pay and charge to them direct the proportion due from them on any claims for loss and damage for $10 and less, without papers other than statement showing claimant, amount, distribution thereof, and way-bill reference. Also we may pay and charge to them direct their proportion of any overcharge claims, supporting the debit with statement showing how the overcharge is determined, full tariff authority, and reference to billing. Errors are subject to correction by recharge before the monthly settlement which is made by draft on agreed date of the succeeding month; after which by special authority.

With certain immediate connections, we have agreements under which we may bill on them for any overcharges paid for their account without previous reference of papers. Errors are subject to correction by recharge and bill subject to draft on agreed date of succeeding month.

### Norfolk & Western Railway Company

The overcharge claims are directly under the supervision of the auditor of receipts, and checking the claims against the records is handled directly by the claim force, as there would be no object in sending these papers from the claim room to be checked up by another force of men in the way-bill or recording departments proper; furthermore, the auditing department starts the overcharge claims and carries them through to a finish, and does the vouchering, the paying, and the rendering of bills for collection against connecting lines for proportions due by them, so that the cost, it is believed, presented on the statement is actually nearer the true cost than many other roads figure it. A considerable portion of the freight claim agent's office force is engaged in tracing and locating "overs" and "shorts," a great portion of which items may never reach voucher shape; nevertheless, it is considered that a proportion of this work is incident to the handling of claims.

### Saint Louis & San Francisco Railroad Company

It is rather difficult to outline briefly our method of handling claims. We practically pay at once in the neighborhood of 50% of our claims, throwing the items in suspense account. All local claims, where other lines are not interested, of $5 and under, are paid immediately upon presentation. In fact, our claim department today is issuing vouchers covering claims presented five days ago. We could dispose of a greater number of claims immediately if it were not for the delay experienced in securing return of such claim papers from connecting lines with authority. We refer a claim to our next connection; they in turn refer it to their connection, and I believe in some instances we incur more expense for telegraphing, postage, and so forth, than the claim proper amounts to.

### Seaboard Air Line Railway

All claims received in this office are promptly recorded and a card sent to each claimant acknowledging claims sent direct to this company, and a card sent to connecting lines acknowledging claims received through that source. These cards show the number under which the claim had been recorded in this office in order to facilitate subsequent correspondence.

Our book record of claims shows the date received, claim number, claimant's name, nature of claim, and amount. When the claim is finally adjusted by voucher, or by authority, or is declined, or withdrawn, this disposition is recorded in the record book. When a claim has been recorded we make what we term a base, which gives a more full description of the claim than is shown in the record book. These bases are filed in boxes, one hundred to a box, and a carbon copy of each endorsement made by us in connection with this claim is fastened to this base.

We keep an alphabetical index of claimants' names and opposite the name we show the number of each claim recorded in favor of that party. In this way we are able to locate all the claims presented by such party for a given period. The record book will show which of these claims are still unadjusted and by referring to the base we find the present whereabouts of the claim and what correspondence has been conducted regarding its adjustment.

Claims, after being recorded, are distributed among investigators; the overcharge claims being divided according to territories and gateways, and according to commodities. Loss and damage claims are divided according to their amounts and importance.

In paying claims after investigation we make vouchers in favor of claimants, or agents, covering claims presented direct to us; these might be termed cash vouchers as they in each instance become a sight draft on our treasurer when properly receipted by payee. In paying our proportion of claims sent us by other lines we issue a draft authority for our proportion of the claim.

Claims paid by our agents are remitted to the comptroller on the first and fifteenth of each month, the agent immediately receiving credit for the total of his list, and the total of these claims is charged to our Claims Suspense Account, all papers being turned over to this office for further handling. These claims are recorded in detail in our suspense record book.

A journal is kept in this office showing all details of entries to various accounts made by this department and this journal is posted each month to the comptroller's ledger.

All authorities from other lines are collected by this office and remittances for same are turned over to our treasurer to credit Claims Receivable Account. Vouchers are prepared in this office in favor of other lines in settlement of claim accounts rendered against this company.

From the above information it will be seen that we are handling considerable accounting work, which is not done by claim departments of most companies. We keep in this office accounts with 283 roads, which relieves the comptroller's office of all details in connection with interline claim accounts.

In connection with our overcharge work we keep a fairly complete file of rates and divisions in order that so far as possible overcharge claims can be adjusted by us without reference to the traffic department.

There is a considerable amount of work handled in this office outside of the actual investigation of claims. During the period in question we recorded 5,908 telegraphic tracers, 1,040 reconsignment files, 1,388 disposition files, 8,834 mail tracers, 10,563 exceptions, 98 wreck files, 50 fire files, and 745 general correspondence files. We made and recorded 4,138 vouchers, and 8,804 authorities, and recorded in our suspense record 29,988 claims.

## Southern Railway Company

Freight claims for overcharges and for losses and damages are presented by claimants in the majority of cases to the local agent, and in other cases direct to the freight claim agent.

If a claim be presented to the agent, sufficient data, such as copy of way-bill, original expense bill and bill of lading, and copy of exception report (if it be for loss or damage), and such other information as may be pertinent or of consequence, is accumulated by the local agent.

If the claim be for overcharge, and the agent is able to reconcile the amount of overcharge claimed or the rate specified in the bill of lading upon which the claim is made with prevailing tariffs or rates, the overcharge is, on receipt of the claim by the agent, refunded by him. Receipt of the claimant is taken for such refund.

If the claim is for an ordinary loss or damage, not exceeding in amount $50, and the agent holds authority of the auditor to pay such claim, after fully establishing the validity of the amount claimed by personally inspecting both goods and invoices, the claim is paid. The original invoice is attached to the claim papers. A claim thus paid by a local agent is remitted to the auditor of station accounts as a credit to his account. On receipt it is examined as to correctness, the agent credited, and "Suspended Claim Account" charged. The claim is then passed to the freight claim agent for investigation as to liability.

If it be found that the liability is with the Southern Railway, the amount of the claim is charged to "Loss and Damage" or "Freight Revenue," as the case may be, and applied to the credit of the "Suspended Claim Account."

Claims filed with agents, which cannot be paid on presentation, are with the necessary supporting papers sent to the freight claim agent for investigation.

Claims filed directly with the freight claim agent are on receipt, after being recorded, numbered, and the claimant advised as to the claim number, thoroughly examined by the freight claim agent and if liability is found beyond all question it is the usual practice for the freight claim agent at that time to issue voucher for the payment of the claim.

If the validity of the claim cannot be at that time established by the freight claim agent, it is placed in course of investigation.

Claims paid on presentation to the freight claim agent, if the liability be with the Southern Railway, are charged to "Loss and Damage" or "Freight Earnings" as the case may be.

If the liability be apparent, but not fixed, the amount of the claim is charged to "Suspense" where it is held until the claim is finally investigated.

The investigation of claims in order to establish both the liability to the claimant and the liability of other carriers is tedious, prolonged, and under present conditions, unsatisfactory.

It frequently occurs that claims for investigation sent to agents, especially those at points of junction with other carriers, to establish the delivery to or receipt from such carriers are seriously delayed.

On the other hand, it frequently occurs that such claims are returned to the freight claim agent with improper or insufficient information, thus further delaying the investigation and causing additional handling of the claim.

This is one of the troubles to which a large percentage of the delays in the adjustment of claims, and incidentally complaints of claimants, is chargeable.

If a claim be for an interline shipment, after accumulating all the data necessary from agents and officials of this company, the claim is sent to the freight claim agent of the next connecting carrier and is by him passed through a similar channel of investigation as that used by the freight claim agent of this company. After completing his investigation, if a third or fourth line be interested, the claim is similarly passed on up the line to the freight claim agent of the last interested carrier in line.

It frequently happens that after going through this process, the claim is returned to the freight claim agent of this company and it is found that information needed for the adjustment of the claim is lacking. The claim is again started on its return journey, thereby causing serious and continued delays.

As the liability of each line is determined an authority for its proportion of the liability, usually in favor of the paying or initial line, is attached to the claim, and when completed the initial line has in its possession authorities to charge other lines with their respective proportions of the amount claimed.

When thus completed a voucher is issued by the freight claim agent in favor of the claimant—if the claim has not been previously paid—to whom payment is made. Vouchers thus made are charged to other interested lines on the authorities issued by them.

Freight claims originating with other carriers in which the Southern Railway is interested are sent to the freight claim agent of the Southern Railway and are investigated by him in a similar manner. If investigation made by the freight claim agent develops liability with this company, an authority to charge it with such liability is attached to the claim.

When issued by the freight claim agent, such authority is recorded by the auditor as a current liability to the debit of "Loss and Damage" or "Freight Revenue," as the case may be.

The papers are then returned to the carrier from whom received, and after the investigation has been completed and the claim paid, the Southern Railway is charged by the paying line with the amount of its authority.

The many intricacies in the handling of freight claims make it almost impossible to intelligently outline a thorough description of the methods followed in the investigation and handling of freight claims. The foregoing is a brief outline of the channels through which freight claims are passed.

The main delay now existing in the investigation of freight claims is due to delays in getting prompt returns of claims from local agents, insufficient information given by agents and freight claim agents, and the numerous times necessary to handle an interline claim during its investigation. Each claim is handled while under investigation an average of five times.

## Exhibit "C"

### BRIEFS OF CERTAIN CLAIMS REVIEWED IN THE OFFICES OF SOME OF THE CARRIERS, AND NOTES ON CLAIMS

### First Case

Claims for $23 loss on flour shipped from a point in Tennessee to a point in North Carolina, via three carriers, A, B, and C. Filed April 28, 1902, with agent at destination, and sent by him to the claim agent of C.

The shipment was made in March, 1902, and the agent at destination made a report that there were 10 barrels of flour short. This report was attached to the claim papers.

The claim was sent by the claim agent of C to the agent at the junction point, for report of the shipment and condition passing that station.

It was returned to the claim agent of C on May 5, with a report that the shipment passed under through seals.

The claim agent of C then sent it to the agent at destination, asking for copy of original way-bill, which was attached and returned on May 9.

The claim agent of C then sent it to a transfer point, requesting report showing correct loading and forwarding.

The agent at the transfer point returned it on May 17, with an exception report showing 10 barrels of flour checked short.

The claim agent of C sent it on May 22 to the claim agent of B, asking him to investigate and advise settlement.

The claim agent of B sent it to the second terminal agent on May 24, asking for advice as to how the shipment checked in passing; and the agent at the terminal of B returned it to the claim agent of B on May 27, with a copy of the exception record showing 10 barrels of flour short.

The claim agent of B then sent it to the agent at the first terminal of B, requesting copy of billing. This was attached, and claim was returned to the claim agent of B on June 2.

The claim agent of B then sent it on June 4 to the claim agent of A, to note and advise settlement. The claim agent of A obtained the usual check in the auditor's office and sent it to the terminal agent of A on June 12 to advise.

The terminal agent of A returned it on July 21, stating that "there was no excess here," and to note that the waybill had been corrected to read 10-96 (meaning 10 sacks of 96 pounds each). (There was a note on the claim that the original bill of lading had 10 barrels of flour, whereas 10 sacks of flour were shipped).

The claim agent of A then sent it to the claim agent of B on July 23, to note and have matter submitted to their agent at destination.

This was done on July 28, with request to advise, and it came back from the agent at destination on July 29 to the claim agent of B, with a copy of the exception attached showing that 10 sacks of flour were over and the statement that the flour had been turned over to a representative of B in accordance with instructions for disposition.

The claim agent of B then sent it to the representative who had sold the flour on July 30, to note the account sales and return, and it came back to the claim agent of B with the statement that 10 sacks of 92 pounds each had been sold on May 20 for $13.50.

The claim agent of B sent it on July 31 to his terminal

agent asking why the over report showed 96-pound sacks when the report of sales showed 92-pound sacks.

The agent returned it to the claim agent of B on August 1, stating that they were 96-pound sacks, and the claim agent of B sent it on August 4 to the representative who had made the sale to advise specifically whether they were 92-pound or 96-pound sacks.

The representative of B returned it on August 6, stating that his record showed that they were 92-pound sacks.

Then the claim agent of B sent it again to the terminal agent of B on September 24, to note the endorsement and advise further.

It came back to the claim agent of B from the agent on September 26, with the statement that the flour was in 96-pound sacks, as was shown on the purchaser's record.

The claim agent of B sent it again, on October 1, to the representative who had made the sale, to note the endorsement of the agent and advise further.

The representative of B sent it back on October 10 to the claim agent of B, saying that he could not state specifically whether or not the flour was in 92-pound or 96-pound sacks, but that the bill stated 92 pounds, which also showed that the flour should have been sold by the barrel, and that therefore the weight of the sacks would make no difference.

The claim agent of B sent it on October 16 to the claim agent of A, advising that this flour came in a car under A's seal and checked over and was sold for $13.50, and because A's agent had knowledge of this fact and did not advise, B expected A to take care of the deficit.

The claim agent of A sent it on October 20 to the point of origin, to note that the trouble was caused by the shipper billing 10 barrels and loading 10 sacks, and requesting that collection be made from the shipper.

The agent returned it to the claim agent of A on October

24, stating that he could not agree that the shipper should make good the difference, that a correction was issued three days after the shipment moved, and that it appeared that the fault was clearly with B in handling the correction.

The claim agent of A then sent it to the claim agent of B on October 29, to note copy of correction issued by the agent showing that the agent at the terminal of B must have had information to enable him to handle the shipment.

The claim agent of B sent it to the second terminal agent on November 6 to note correction and advise disposition.

The agent returned it on November 7 to the claim agent of B, stating that the correction issued was not handled by him and that the billing of C was not taken into his account.

The claim agent of B then sent it back to the agent at the first terminal on November 10, to note and advise, and the agent returned it to the claim agent of B on November 11, stating that this correction was reissued by him on March 8, five days after it was issued at the point of origin, and that the agent at point of origin was at fault in not notifying the agent at the other terminal of B of the fact that the flour was over.

The claim agent of B then sent it to the claim agent of A on November 26, stating that the correction was handled with reasonable promptness and that the trouble occurred with the shipper, also with the agent at the point of origin in not notifying the agent at the terminal of B, and under the circumstances the deficit should be borne by the shipper or by A.

The claim agent of A then sent it to the agent at the point of origin on November 28, to note and advise, and the agent returned it to the claim agent of A on December

11, stating that as soon as the discrepancy was discovered a correction was issued and that a wire had been sent to the agent at the terminal relative to the error; also that he issued the correction on March 3, which was reissued by the agent of B on March 8, and that the consignees had filed the claim on April 25, one month and 17 days after the correction was issued. Under these circumstances he could not see why the shipper should make good the deficit caused by the connecting line's error.

The claim agent of A then sent it back to the claim agent of B on December 4, to note that the shippers took prompt action, and that in his opinion they should not be called on to sustain the loss. Suggested that the way to adjust the claim was for all lines to pay their revenue proportion.

The claim agent of B sent it to the claim agent of C on December 15, to note and advise if settlement suggested by A was satisfactory.

The claim agent of C returned it to the claim agent of B on December 29, stating that as the shipment was never delivered to C he could not authorize for any part of the claim.

The claim agent of B then sent it to the claim agent of A on March 3, 1903, to note reply of the claim agent of C.

The claim agent of A returned it to the claim agent of B March 7, with authority for 50% of the loss.

The claim agent of B then returned it to the claim agent of A on March 17, stating that the authority attached would not enable C to adjust their claim, and requesting an increase.

The claim agent of A returned it to the claim agent of B on March 24, stating that as B seemed to be as much at fault as A, the authority of March 7 for 50% of the loss should be allowed to stand as rendered.

The claim agent of B then returned it to the claim agent

of A on May 8, stating that the fault was entirely with A, and insisting on authority for the full amount.

The claim agent of A returned it to the claim agent of B on May 14, saying that B contributed to the negligence.

The claim agent of B sent it back to the claim agent of A on May 20, denying that they contributed to the negligence and asking for full authority for the amount of the claim.

The claim agent of A sent it again to the claim agent of B on June 18, acknowledging that the original error was made by A, and stating that the agent at the point of origin discovered the error and issued a correction on March 3, 1902, which was not reissued by the agent of B until March 8, 1902, and that the claim was not filed until a month and 17 days after correction was issued by B, and that the delay in handling the correction by B contributed to the error; therefore B should participate.

The claim agent of B then sent it to the claim agent of A (date omitted), stating that the correction was received and promptly handled, and insisting on authority for the whole amount of the claim.

The claim agent of A then returned it to the claim agent of B on November 25, stating that there was no doubt at all that B contributed and that the 50% authorized should stand.

The claim agent of B returned it again to the claim agent of A on December 4, requesting authority and stating that A was liable.

The claim agent of A sent it to the agent at the point of origin on December 9, stating that the shipper seemed to be as much in error as A, and requesting that the shipper be asked to stand one-half of claim.

The agent at the point of origin sent it to the claim agent of A on December 28, stating that the papers did not show that there had been any effort on the part of the second terminal agent of B to move the shipment to destination after the correction had been handled by the first terminal agent of B, and suggesting that before the matter be taken up with the shipper it should be referred to B for investigation.

The claim agent of A sent it to the claim agent of B on December 29, to note and advise.

The claim agent of B sent it to the agent at the terminal on December 31, to note and advise.

The agent at the terminal returned it to the claim agent of B on January 2, 1904, saying that he had not received or handled the correction referred to, and that the flour was turned over to the representative for disposition on April 26, 1902.

The claim agent of B then sent it to the claim agent of A on January 5, to note result of investigation and authorize for the full amount of claim.

The claim agent of A sent it back to the claim agent of B on January 7, stating that the agent at one terminal of B received the correction on March 8, 1902, and that the agent at the other terminal of B did not handle it at all; therefore B contributed to the error and should pay one-half.

The claim agent of B then sent it to the auditor of B on January 12 for a report of the original correction. The auditor returned it to the claim agent on January 15, stating that it was solid billing, and that the agent at the first terminal might have mailed the correction ahead to the agent at the second terminal.

The claim agent of B sent it back to the claim agent of A on January 22, stating that A was liable and insisting on authority for the full amount.

The claim agent of A sent it back to the agent at the point of origin on January 25, to see if the shipper would not join in the payment of the claim.

The agent at the point of origin returned it to the claim agent of A on January 30, 1904, advising that the matter had been taken up with the shipper in person without success, and with letter attached from the shipper to the agent dated January 30, advising that instructions had been issued one week after the shipment to correct billing. The shipper refused to participate in the claim.

The claim agent of A then sent it back to the agent at the point of origin on February 8, to note that he had knowledge that the shipper had been one week in effecting the change in the billing, and requesting that the shipper be asked to pay one-half of the claim.

The agent returned it to the claim agent of A on February 16, stating that the fault lay with the agent at the terminal of B in not handling the information properly, and that he did not believe that the shipper contributed to the negligence.

The claim agent of A sent it to the agent at the point of origin on February 19, stating that the shipper delayed a week in effecting the change in billing instructions and asking that the shipper participate.

The agent then returned it to the claim agent of A on March 8, to note a letter attached from the shipper. The shipper wrote to the agent on March 4, stating that the shipper was forced to collect the amount by suit from the consignee, and that this suit had cost $9.56, which amount had been charged to the consignee. The shipper was willing to apply 50% of this claim, or $4.75, in settlement with the consignee, if acceptable to him.

The claim agent of A then sent it back to the claim agent of B on March 9 to note, and the claim agent of B sent it to the claim agent of C on March 12, to note the letter of the claim agent of A and advise.

The claim agent of C returned it to the claim agent of B on March 21, stating that he had nothing whatever to do with the manner in which shippers collected their accounts and insisting on authority for the net proceeds of the sale and also for the balance of the claim.

The claim agent of B then sent it to the claim agent of C on March 29, stating that this claim should be settled, after explanation of consignee, by payment of the amount, less $4.75, which had to be credited to his account by the shipper, and admitting no liability on the part of B, B declining to pass authority for part of the claim.

The claim agent of C sent it to the claim agent of B on April 2, stating that the claimant would not accept anything less than the full amount of the claim, and requesting authority to be returned, as this matter had been standing about two years.

The claim agent of B sent it to the claim agent of C on April 5, requesting that he attempt to settle the claim as previously suggested.

The claim agent of C sent it to the agent at destination on April 16, to note papers and attempt to have claim reduced in accordance with suggestion.

The agent at destination returned it to the claim agent of C on April 27, to note letter of claimant attached. The letter of the claimant was addressed to the agent at destination on April 27, declining to reduce claim 50% of attorney's fees.

The claim agent of C then sent it to the claim agent of B on April 28, to note that claimant refused to reduce the claim, and requesting authority.

The claim agent of B sent it back to the claim agent of A on May 6, to note the correspondence attached from the claim agent of C and to pass full authority.

The claim agent of A sent it to the agent at the point of origin on May 9, to note that the arrangement suggested by the shipper could not be made, and to please secure the shipper's check for the deficit.

The agent returned it to the claim agent of A on May 17, to note reply of shipper, in which it was stated that although the shipper had made an error, notice within a week to correct was sufficient to have allowed proper correction. There was a letter attached from the shipper to the agent at the point of origin dated May 13, declining to bear any part of the loss.

The claim agent of A then sent it to the agent at the point of origin on May 27, stating that A would have to assume the claim, but in future an indemnity letter should be secured from shippers if they wish to make changes in bills of lading, unless such changes are requested within 24 hours.

The agent returned it to the claim agent of A on June 3, stating that the instructions would be carried out.

The claim agent of A then sent it to the claim agent of B on June 6, stating that they would stand proportion on revenue basis, all lines joining, of one-half of claim, the other one-half to be individually paid by A.

The claim agent of B then sent it to the claim agent of C on June 15, to note the proposition of A, and stating that B did not appear to be interested.

The claim agent of C returned it to the claim agent of B on July 12, stating that they wanted authority for $23 and that nothing less would do. Unless authority was attached the claim would be prepared for arbitration. They had too much work to do to be bothered with this small matter.

The claim agent of B then returned it to the claim agent of A on July 19, to note result of investigation.

The claim agent of A sent it to the claim agent of B on July 21, with authority to charge A with $9.50, the amount of claim less the amount received from the sale of shipment.

The claim agent of B then sent it to the claim agent

of C on July 25, with the authority of the connecting lines attached, and request to please charge correct.

It will be noted that settlement was not effected for about 2½ years. There were 109 pieces of paper attached to the claim. This claim was filed April 28, 1902. At that time it was known that the shipment was short at the destination. An inquiry was sent to the connecting lines on May 22. On May 27 the claim agent of B was advised that 10 barrels were checked short at the second terminal. This information was sufficient to justify the payment of the claim and was ascertained within five days of the time that the inquiry was sent to the claim agent of B. The actual sale of the consignment, it having been checked over by B, was made on May 5, 1902, and much correspondence followed over the question as to whether the sacks weighed 92 or 96 pounds. The facts in regard to the error that occasioned the check of over, the sale of the consignment and the shortage at the destination were all disclosed within a few days after the papers were sent to the carriers in interest. In the meantime the claimant had not been paid; the shipper had brought suit againt the consignee to recover the value of the flour at an expense in attorney's fees of $9.56, which he had charged to the consignee; and B, the intermediate carrier, though having no interest, had sold the flour and held the proceeds of sale, $13.50, awaiting settlement of the claim.

The papers passed 24 times back and forth between the claim agents of B and A without disclosing any material new evidence.

In a lot of 10 claims taken at random in which the first case was found, there was another case involving $57.50 on a shipment from a point in Massachusetts to a point in Alabama. This case had 193 pieces of paper attached and would have shown nearly twice as many movements as the case already cited, but it was thought to be less applicable to the point at issue because a considerable part of the movement was outside of the southeastern territory. It should be said, however, in this latter case, that practically all the facts necessary for the immediate disposition of the claim were disclosed within five days of the first movement to each of the carriers interested. The claim was filed in 1900, and still remains unsettled.

The others in the lot of 10 claims were less striking, but disclosed, to a greater or less extent, the present cumbersome methods of handling claims.

## Second Case

Shipments from a point north of the Ohio River outside of the southeastern territory to a point in Mississippi, via three carriers, A, B, and C. Reference to movements to and from agents is omitted to avoid the burden of voluminous detail.

Claim was filed with the agent of C at destination March 14, 1903, for $464.75, and sent to the claim agent of C on April 12, 1903. The shipment had been made in February, 1903. Investigation and correspondence resulted, after a sale of the salvage had been made and credited on the account, in reducing the claim to $272.11. This amount was established on May 3, 1903. The records showed that the shipment had gone through without breaking bulk and was damaged by moisture.

The papers were sent by the claim agent of C to the claim agent of B on May 11, 1903.

The claim agent of B made an investigation of the case through agents, and sent the papers to the claim agent of A on July 27, 1903.

The claim agent of A made an investigation and returned the papers to the claim agent of B on August 15, 1903, declined.

The claim agent of B sent the papers to the claim agent of C August 19, declining participation.

The claim agent of C again returned the papers to B on August 24, showing that the damage resulted from moisture en route that could not be located, and again requesting participation.

Then the claim agent of B sent the papers to the claim agent of A on August 29, to note.

The claim agent of A made a further investigation, similar to the one made at first, and returned the papers to the claim agent of B October 26, declined.

The claim agent of B then again returned them to the claim agent of C on November 9, declined.

The claim agent of C then sent them back to the claim agent of B on November 14, with a similar presentation to that of August 24.

Again the claim agent of B sent the papers to the claim agent of A December 22, to note.

The claim agent of A returned them to the claim agent of B on February 25, 1904, again declined.

The claim agent of B then sent them to the claim agent of C on April 4, 1904, requesting the handling of papers direct between C and A, stating that B would agree to stand a proportion if a *pro rata* of the three carriers concerned could be agreed upon.

Then the claim agent of C sent the papers direct to the claim agent of A on April 6, calling attention to the proposition made by the claim agent of B.

A returned the papers to C on June 16, 1904, again declining to participate.

Then the claim agent of C sent them back to the claim agent of A on July 2, with another appeal.

The claim agent of A returned them again to the claim agent of C on August 6, declined.

On October 10, the claim agent of C wrote a personal letter to the head of the traffic department of A, explaining the case and expressing regret to have to trouble the head of the traffic department with a claim matter; but desired to bring the injustice of the persistent declinations of the claim department to the head of the traffic department, so that proper attention might be given to the case.

Meanwhile there was added to the claim papers correspondence from a representative of C, complaining of the delay in the settlement of the claim and stating that the consignee had become so dissatisfied that he had changed the routing of other freight and was threatening suit if not paid immediately.

The claim agent of C then authorized the claim paid on October 10, 1904, the amount to be charged to suspense.

The head of the traffic department of A returned the papers to the claim agent of C on November 14, 1904, with a short letter acknowledging the liability and agreeing to participate, giving authority to charge A with a proportion on mileage basis.

The claim papers were then about to be sent by the claim agent of C to the claim agent of B to get authority for its proportion on a mileage basis.

All the information obtainable in regard to this shipment and the damage that occurred was found in the papers on the first move to each of the carriers interested; so that the carrier making the settlement knew all that was ever known regarding the loss at the time the initial investigation was made. There is no reason why the claim should not have been paid immediately after the initial investigation and a proper distribution made of the amount at that time. This would have satisfied the claimant, and disposed of the amount as between the carriers. As a matter of fact, it took from May 11, 1903, to August 19, 1903, to get complete information back to C from the first investigation with the carriers interested. The papers were under investigation with B from May 11 to July 27, and with A from July 27 to August 15, and were delayed four days in being returned from B to C.

### Third Case

Shipments of trunks from a point in Georgia to a point in Indian Territory, via three carriers, A, B, and C, damaged on the line of carrier C. The claim was filed with the claim agent of A July 14, 1903, for $42.20, and was received by the claim agent of B August 15, 1903.

Again, many of the movements are omitted to save voluminous detail.

The claim agent of B made an exhaustive examination at terminals and transfer points and found the shipment had passed that line in good order.

The papers were sent to the claim agent of C on April 5, 1904, where the investigation with the agents and the copy of the over, short, and damage report showed the damage to have occurred on C's line.

The consignment was sold by C and the papers were returned by the claim agent of C to the claim agent of B on May 16, 1904, asking what disposition should be made of the matter.

The papers were returned by the claim agent of B to the claim agent of C, pointing out the fact that the loss occurred on the line of carrier C and that the whole of the claim was a charge against that line; whereupon the claim agent of C returned the papers on August 4, 1904, to the claim agent of B authorizing a charge of $25.

The papers were then returned to the claim agent of A, and the claim agent of A sent them to the agent at the point of origin to confer with the claimant and ascertain if $25 would be accepted. The claimant refused to accept $25 in settlement of a total loss of $42.20, and the agent at the point of origin returned the papers to the claim agent of A, who, in turn, sent them back to the claim agent of B.

The claim agent of B then sent them back again to the claim agent of C, showing that the shipper had declined the offer of $25, and asking for authority to charge that line with the full amount; whereupon the claim agent of C authorized on November 18, 1904, for the full amount.

This case was found with the claim agent of B about to be sent to the claim agent of A with authority to pay the claim and to charge all of the amount against carrier C.

There were 71 pieces of paper attached to the claim and 22 movements took place to and from carrier B, the intermediate line that really had nothing to do with the case and knew this from its initial investigation, which required but a few days. Practically a year and one-half was spent in settling a claim that should have been disposed of very easily within a month.

There was another claim in this lot of 10 for loss on live stock, $6,600, filed July 2, 1902. The carrier to which the claim had been presented compromised with the claimant on November 5, 1902, reducing it from $6,600 to $1,500.

The three carriers made separate investigations, simultaneously, commencing August 1, 1902, to ascertain the facts in regard to the shipment. In one case it took a month and 13 days; in another case, a month and 16 days; and in the other case, 2 months and 16 days. The correspondence between the lines has been continuous and at this time there are 286 pieces of paper attached and no agreement as to distribution of the amount has yet been reached.

In this complicated and difficult case, all the facts disclosed were known within two months and a half after the time the original investigation was commenced by each carrier, so that at the outside the whole case could have been disposed of and the distribution made within that time.

### Fourth Case

Claim for $13.53 loss on salt fish shipped from a point in New England to a point in Mississippi, November 1, 1902, via seven carriers, A, B, C, D, E, F, and G. Filed with the general agent of carrier C February 9, 1903, and sent by the claim agent of C to the first terminal agent on February 13.

The papers came back to the claim agent of C, with no exceptions, on February 24 and were sent by the claim agent of C to the second terminal agent on February 28, and were again returned on March 4, unable to locate.

On March 10, the papers were sent to the commercial agent at the second terminal of carrier C and were returned to the claim agent of C on March 27, showing the delivery to carrier D, and also to carrier E, on November 12, 1902.

The claim agent of C sent the papers to the claim agent of E, on April 1, to trace delivery.

On April 8, 1903, the claim agent of E sent the papers to the first terminal (addressed by mistake to a station of the same name in another state, whence they were returned on April 9, and were remailed to the first terminal in the proper state April 15), and they were returned to the claim agent with a note that carrier D had been recharged and shipment returned November 15, 1902.

The claim agent of carrier E then sent the papers to the claim agent of D April 17, 1903, to note.

The claim agent of D sent the papers to his first terminal on April 24, 1903, to show delivery.

The papers were returned from the agent at the first terminal on April 25, showing delivery to an eighth carrier, H, on a mem-bill November 24, 1902.

The claim agent of D then sent the papers on April 29 to the claim agent of H to show delivery.

The claim agent of H sent the papers to the agent of H at the first terminal, being the same terminal as the first terminal of D, to furnish the information.

The papers were then returned on May 18, showing forwarding on November 24 to the second terminal of carrier H.

The claim agent of H then sent the papers to the agent at the second terminal, to show delivery.

The papers were returned June 29, showing delivery to carrier E, without exception, November 26, 1902.

Then the claim agent of H sent the papers to the claim agent of E July 31, 1903. (Meantime two letters had been attached tracing for the claim.)

On August 17 the claim agent of E sent the papers to the agent at the transfer point.

The papers were returned to the claim agent of E on August 21, showing billing to the connecting point with carrier G.

The claim agent of E then sent the papers to the agent at the junction point for the record at that station.

The papers were returned August 31, showing delivery to the last carrier, G, without exception, on December 2, 1902.

On September 3, 1903, the claim agent of E sent the papers to the claim agent of G to show delivery.

On September 11 the claim agent of G sent the papers to the first terminal agent for record.

The papers were returned to the claim agent on September 14, showing forwarding to destination, without exception, on December 11, 1902.

On September 25 the claim agent of G sent the papers to the agent at destination to show delivery.

The papers were returned on September 26, showing that the consignment was damaged and had been sold for 75 cents, on the authority of the claim agent of G, January 16, 1903.

On October 28, 1903, the claim agent of G sent the papers back to the claim agent of E, saying that the shipper should accept the proceeds of the sale in settlement of the claim.

Then the claim agent of E sent the papers back to the claim agent of C on October 31, 1903, with a note: "Will you accept proceeds of sale?"

The claim agent of C sent the papers on November 3,

1903, to the claim agent of D to pay the claim or have carrier E participate.

The agent of D sent to agent at second terminal November 12, for full record.

The papers were returned with note of billing, November 18.

The claim agent of D then returned the papers to the claim agent of C on January 15, 1904, to take up with carrier E.

The claim agent of C returned the papers to the claim agent of D on January 26, 1904, suggesting basis for settlement with D, E, and G.

The claim agent of D then sent the papers to the first terminal agent on February 1, 1904, for information.

The papers were returned on February 2, giving data, with the note: "Error in Loading."

Claim agent of D then sent the papers to the claim agent of H on February 4, 1904, to participate, on account of delay.

The claim agent of H sent them to his first terminal agent on March 7, for information, and they were returned March 15, 1904, with the statement that there had been no delay at his station.

Then the claim agent of H sent the papers to the claim agent of D March 22, declining.

The claim agent of D then again returned the papers to the claim agent of H on March 25, asking for further information, and the claim agent of H again returned them to the claim agent of D on March 28, declining.

The claim agent of D then sent the papers on April 4, 1904, to the claim agent of E, requesting authority.

The claim agent of E then sent the papers to the claim agent of G April 27, to note.

The claim agent of G sent the papers to the agent at destination point on June 22, 1904, for his record, and the

| | |
|---|---|
| Number of Interline Loss and Damage Claims Received: | |
| From Other Carriers (48.76%) .......... | 124,385 |
| Originating with Each Carrier (51.24%) .. | 130,718 |
| Total Interline Loss and Damage Claims Received ................ | 255,103 |
| Percentage of Interline Loss and Damage to Total Interline Claims .............. | 45.53 |
| Total Number of Interline Claims Received: | |
| From Other Carriers .................. | 281,523 |
| Originating with Each Carrier ........... | 278,793 |
| Total Interline Claims Received ..... | 560,316 |
| Percentage of Claims Received from Other Carriers to Total Interline Claims ...... | 50.24 |
| Percentage of Claims Originating on Each Line to Total Interline Claims ........ | 49.76 |
| Number of Clerks in Claims Department: | |
| At the Beginning of the Period .......... | 310 |
| At the End of the Period ............... | 326 |
| Pay-Roll of the Claims Department: | |
| At the Beginning of the Period (per month) | $18,026.71 |
| At the End of the Period (per month) .... | $19,207.50 |
| Average Number of Employees for the Year... | 313½ |
| Average Pay-Roll for the Year .............. | $220,745.88 |
| Average Cost of Handling Each Claim Received ............................cents, | 28.33 |
| Highest Average Cost of Handling Each Claim Received by Any One Carrier ........cents, | 46.52 |
| Lowest Average Cost of Handling Each Claim Received by Any One Carrier ........cents, | 17.09 |
| Estimated Amount of Time Devoted to Interline Claims in the Aggregate Greater than That Devoted to Local Claims ........... | 2 to 3 Times |

Estimating that it costs three (3) times as much to handle an interline as it does a local claim:

Average Cost per Claim:

| | |
|---|---|
| Local ..................... cents, | 11.62 |
| Interline .................. cents, | 34.86 |

Average Cost:

| | |
|---|---|
| Local .......................... | $25,423.91 |
| Interline ........................ | $195,321.97 |
| Percentage of Average Cost of Local to Total Cost of Claims ................ | 11.52 |
| Percentage of Average Cost of Interline to Total Cost of Claims ................ | 88.48 |

Estimating that it costs two and one-half (2½) times as much to handle an interline as it does a local claim:

Average Cost per Claim:

| | |
|---|---|
| Local ..................... cents, | 13.63 |
| Interline .................. cents, | 34.07 |

Average Cost:

| | |
|---|---|
| Local .......................... | $29,821.75 |
| Interline ........................ | $190,924.13 |
| Percentage of Average Cost of Local to Total Cost of Claims ................ | 13.51 |
| Percentage of Average Cost of Interline to Total Cost of Claims ................ | 86.49 |

Estimating that it costs two (2) times as much to handle an interline as it does a local claim:

Average Cost per Claim:

| | |
|---|---|
| Local ..................... cents, | 16.48 |
| Interline .................. cents, | 32.96 |

Average Cost:

| | |
|---|---|
| Local .......................... | $36,059.33 |
| Interline ........................ | $184,686.55 |
| Percentage of Average Cost of Local to Total Cost of Claims ................ | 16.34 |
| Percentage of Average Cost of Interline to Total Cost of Claims ................ | 83.66 |

## Exhibit "E"

### CLAIMS INVOLVING AMOUNTS OF $1 AND UNDER, $2.50 AND UNDER, $5 AND UNDER, AND $10 AND UNDER—BASED UPON 13,229 CLAIMS HANDLED IN THE OFFICES OF SEVEN OF THE CARRIERS

| | |
|---|---|
| Total Number of Claims Received by Seven of the Carriers | 13,229 |
| Total Amount of Claims | $251,160.14 |
| Average per Claim | $18.99 |
| Claims of One ($1) Dollar and Under: | |
| Number of Claims | 1,508 |
| Percentage of Number | 11.40 |
| Amount | $921.83 |
| Percentage of Amount | .37 |
| Average per Claim .....cents, | .61 |
| Claims of Two and one-half ($2.50) Dollars and Under: | |
| Number of Claims | 4,091 |
| Percentage of Number | 30.92 |
| Amount | $5,400.00 |
| Percentage of Amount | 2.15 |
| Average per Claim | $1.32 |
| Claims of Five ($5) Dollars and Under: | |
| Number of Claims | 6,555 |
| Percentage of Number | 49.55 |
| Amount | $14,450.09 |
| Percentage of Amount | 5.75 |
| Average per Claim | $2.21 |
| Claims of Ten ($10) Dollars and Under: | |
| Number of Claims | 8,812 |
| Percentage of Number | 66.61 |
| Amount | $30,466.10 |
| Percentage of Amount | 12.13 |
| Average per Claim | $3.46 |

## Exhibit "F"

### NAMES OF CARRIERS IN THE SOUTHEASTERN TERRITORY AND APPROXIMATE MILEAGE AS SHOWN BY THE OFFICIAL GUIDE, NOT INCLUDING LINES OF LESS THAN 11 MILES IN LENGTH, NOR ABOUT 200 LINES OF SHORT MILEAGE, SUCH AS TERMINALS, LOGGING, COAL, AND PRIVATE ROADS

APPROXIMATE

| Name of Carrier | Mileage Shown by the Official Guide | Location of General Office, Etc. |
|---|---|---|
| Aberdeen & Asheboro Ry... | 82 | Aberdeen, N. C. |
| Aberdeen & Rock Fish R. R. | 44 | Aberdeen, N. C. |
| *Alabama Great Southern R. R. | 309 | Birmingham, Ala. (Q. & C. Route—Southern) |
| Alabama & Mississippi R. R. | 18 | Vinegar Bend, Ala. |
| *Alabama & Vicksburg Ry... | 142 | Jackson, Miss. (Q. & C. Route—Southern) |
| Albany & Northern Ry. .... | 35 | Albany, Ga. |
| Alcolu R. R. | 20 | Alcolu, S. C. |
| Ashland Coal & Iron Ry. .. | 22 | Ashland, Ky. |
| *Atlanta & Birmingham Air Line Ry. | 121 | Portsmouth, Va. (S. A. L.) |
| †Atlanta & West Point R. R. | 87 | Atlanta, Ga., (L. & N.—A. C. L.) |
| *Atlanta, Knoxville & Northern Ry. | 231 | Knoxville, Tenn. (L. & N.) |
| Atlantic & Birmingham R. R. | 332 | Waycross, Ga. |
| Atlantic & North Carolina R. R. | 95 | Goldsboro, N. C. |
| †Atlantic Coast Line R. R... | 4,173 | Wilmington, N. C. |
| *Augusta Southern R. R. ... | 83 | Augusta, Ga. (Southern) |
| Bainbridge Northern R. R. | 32 | Bainbridge, Ga. |
| Berkeley Railroad | 20 | Chicoea, S. C. |
| Bessemer & Southwestern R. R. | 11 | Bessemer, Ala. |
| Birmingham & Atlantic R. R. | 53 | Talladega, Ala. |

*Affiliated with those now identified with movement for revising plan.
†Now identified with movement for revising plan.

| Name of Carrier | Mileage Shown by the Official Guide | Location of General Office, Etc. |
|---|---|---|
| *Birmingham Southern R. R. | 21 | Birmingham, Ala. (L. & N.—Southern) |
| *Blue Ridge Ry. .......... | 44 | Greenville, S. C. (Southern) |
| Cairo & Kanawha Valley R. R. .................. | 18 | Parkersburg, W. Va. |
| Caldwell & Northern R. R. | 11 | Lenoir, N. C. |
| Cape Fear & Northern Ry. | 40 | Apex, N. C. |
| Carolina & Northwestern Ry. .................. | 110 | Chester, S. C. |
| Carolina Northern R. R. .. | 41 | Marion, S. C. |
| Carrabelle, Tallahassee & Georgia R. R. .......... | 50 | Tallahassee, Fla. (Georgia, Florida & Alabama) |
| Carrollton Short Line Ry. | 21 | Carrollton, Ala. |
| Carthage R. R. ........... | 19 | Carthage, N. C. |
| †Central of Georgia Ry. .... | 1,867 | Savannah, Ga. |
| *Charleston & Western Carolina Ry. ........... | 340 | Augusta, Ga. (A. C. L.) |
| Chattahoochee Valley Ry... | 17 | West Point, Ga. |
| Chattanooga Southern R. R. | 99 | Chattanooga, Tenn. |
| Chesapeake & Nashville Ry. | 47 | Gallatin, Tenn. |
| †Chesapeake & Ohio Ry. .... | 1,684 | Richmond, Va. (Penn.) |
| Chesapeake Western Ry. .. | 41 | Harrisonburg, Va. |
| Chesterfield & Lancaster R. R. ................ | 37 | Cheraw, S. C. |
| *Cincinnati, New Orleans & Texas Pacific Ry. ...... | 338 | Cincinnati, O. (Q. & C. Route—Southern) |
| Coal & Coke Ry. ........ | 133 | Elkins, W. Va. |
| Coal River & Western Ry... | 22 | Charleston, W. Va. |
| Columbia, Newberry & Laurens R. R. .......... | 75 | Columbia, S. C. |
| Conway Coast & Western R. R. .................. | 15 | Conway, S. C. |
| Covington, Flemingsburg & Ashland R. R. .......... | 17 | Flemingsburg, Ky. |
| *Danville & Western Ry. ... | 83 | Danville, Va. (Southern) |
| Darien & Western R. R. ... | 31 | Darien, Ga. |
| Dry Fork R. R. .......... | 30 | Hendricks, W. Va. |
| Durham & Charlotte R. R. | 37 | Gulf, N. C. |
| East Carolina Ry. ........ | 26 | Tarboro, N. C. |
| East Louisiana R. R. ..... | 36 | Covington, La. |
| East Tennessee & Western North Carolina R. R..... | 34 | Johnson City, Tenn. |

*Affiliated with those now identified with movement for revising plan.
†Now identified with movement for revising plan.

| Name of Carrier | Mileage Shown by the Official Guide | Location of General Office, Etc. |
|---|---|---|
| Eastern Kentucky Ry. .... | 36 | Riverton, Ky. |
| Ellaville, Westlake & Jennings R. R. ........ | 30 | Westlake, Fla. |
| Farmville & Powhatan R. R. | 93 | Richmond, Va. |
| Fitzgerald, Ocmulgee & Red Bluff Ry. .......... | 15 | Fitzgerald, Ga. |
| Flint River & Northeastern R. R. ................ | 24 | Pelham, Ga. |
| Florida & Georgia Ry. .... | 30 | White Springs, Fla. |
| †Florida East Coast Ry. .... | 503 | St. Augustine, Fla. |
| *Florida West Shore Ry. ... | 64 | Plant City, Fla. (S. A. L.) |
| Frankfort & Cincinnati Ry. | 41 | Frankfort, Ky. |
| Gainesville & Gulf Ry. .... | 48 | Gainesville, Fla. |
| Gainesville Midland Ry. .. | 55 | Gainesville, Ga. |
| Garbutt & Donovan Short Line Ry. .............. | 14 | Lyons, Ga. |
| Georgetown & Western R. R. ................ | 36 | Georgetown, S. C. |
| †Georgia Railroad ........ | 324 | Augusta, Ga. |
| Georgia Eastern Ry. ...... | 18 | Bainbridge, Ga. |
| Georgia, Florida & Alabama Ry. .................. | 106 | Bainbridge, Ga. |
| Georgia Northern Ry. .... | 63 | Moultrie, Ga. |
| *Georgia So. & Florida Ry. | 395 | Macon, Ga. (Southern) |
| Glade Creek & Raleigh R. R. ................ | 15 | Raleigh, W. Va. |
| Glenn Springs R. R. ...... | 16 | Glenn Springs, S. C. |
| Gulf & Ship Island R. R. .. | 261 | Gulfport, Miss. |
| Hampton & Branchville R. R. ................ | 22 | Hampton, S. C. |
| *Harriman & Northeastern R. R. ............... | 20 | Cincinnati, Ohio (Southern) |
| Hawkinsville & Florida So. Ry. .................. | 55 | Hawkinsville, Ga. |
| Holly River & Addison Ry. | 34 | Grafton, W. Va. |
| †Illinois Central R. R. .... | 4,325 | Chicago, Ill. |
| Kanawha & Coal River Ry. | 13 | Spring Hill, W. Va. |
| Kanawha & Michigan Ry... | 177 | Toledo, Ohio (T. & O. C.) |
| †Kansas City, Memphis & Birmingham R. R. ..... | 286 | St. Louis, Mo. (Frisco System) |
| Knoxville & Bristol Ry. ... | 40 | Knoxville, Tenn. |
| LaFayette Ry. .......... | 22 | LaFayette, Ala. |

*Affiliated with those now identified with movement for revising plan.
†Now identified with movement for revising plan.

| Name of Carrier | Mileage Shown by the Official Guide | Location of General Office, Etc. |
|---|---|---|
| Lancaster & Chester Ry. .. | 29 | Lancaster, S. C. |
| Lexington & Eastern Ry. .. | 94 | Lexington, Ky. |
| Licking River R. R. ...... | 30 | Yale, Ky. |
| Little Kanawha R. R. .... | 30 | Parkersburg, W. Va. |
| Liberty White R. R. ...... | 18 | McComb City, Miss. |
| Linville River Ry. ....... | 13 | Saginaw, N. C. |
| Live Oak & Gulf Ry. ...... | 20 | Live Oak, Fla. |
| Louisiana Southern Ry..... | 46 | New Orleans, La. |
| Louisville & Atlantic R. R. | 101 | Versailles, Ky. |
| †Louisville & Nashville R. R. | 3,679 | Louisville, Ky. |
| *Louisville & Wadley R. R. | 11 | Louisville, Ga. (Cent. of Ga.) |
| *Louisville, Henderson & St. Louis Ry. ........... | 200 | Louisville, Ky. (L. & N.) |
| Mount Airy & Eastern Ry. | 19 | Mount Airy, N. C. |
| *Macon & Birmingham Ry. | 105 | Macon, Ga. (Southern) |
| *Macon, Dublin & Savannah R. R. ................. | 92 | Macon, Ga. (A. C. L.) |
| Manistee & Repton R. R. .. | 19 | Manistee, Ala. |
| Marion & Rye Valley Ry. .. | 20 | Marion, Va. |
| Midville, Swainsboro & Red Bluff R. R. ............ | 20 | Swainsboro, Ga. |
| Millen & Southwestern R. R. ................. | 55 | Monte, Ga. |
| Mississippi Central R. R. .. | 55 | Hattiesburg, Miss. |
| *Mobile & Ohio R. R. ...... | 913 | Mobile, Ala. (Southern) |
| Mobile, Jackson & Kansas City R. R. ............ | 260 | Mobile, Ala. |
| Nashville & Sparks R. R... | 12 | Massee, Ga. |
| †Nashville, Chattanooga & St. Louis Ry. .......... | 1,195 | Nashville, Tenn. (L. & N.) |
| Natchez, Columbia & Mobile R. R. ........... | 26 | Norfield, Miss. |
| *New Orleans & Northeastern R. R. ................. | 196 | New Orleans, La. (Q. & C. Route—Southern) |
| Norfolk & Southern R. R. | 159 | Norfolk, Va. |
| †Norfolk & Western Ry. Co. | 1,722 | Roanoke, Va. |
| *Northern Alabama Ry. .... | 115 | New York (Southern) |
| Ohio & Kentucky Ry. ..... | 27 | Cannel City, Ky. |
| Pensacola, Alabama & Tenn. R. R. ................. | 23 | Pensacola, Fla. |
| Porters Creek & Gauley R. R. ................. | 30 | Porter, W. Va. |

*Affiliated with those now identified with movement for revising plan.
†Now identified with movement for revising plan.

| Name of Carrier | Mileage Shown by the Official Guide | Location of General Office, Etc. |
|---|---|---|
| Potomac, Fredericksburg & Piedmont R. R. ........ | 38 | Fredericksburg, Va. |
| Raleigh & Cape Fear Ry. .. | 35 | Raleigh, N. C. |
| Red River Valley R. R. ... | 14 | Rothwell, Ky. |
| *Richmond, Fredericksburg & Potomac R. R. ....... | 90 | Richmond, Va. (A. C. L.—S. A. L.—B. & O.—C. & O.—Penn.—Southern) |
| Sardis & Delta R. R. ...... | 33 | Sardis, Miss. |
| *Savannah & Statesboro Ry. | 53 | Savannah, Ga. (S. A. L.) |
| †Seaboard Air Line Ry. .... | 2,611 | Portsmouth, Va. |
| South & Western Ry. ..... | 64 | Bristol, Va. |
| South Georgia & West Coast Ry. .................. | 77 | Quitman, Ga. |
| †Southern Ry. ............ | 7,156 | Washington, D. C. |
| Stillmore Air Line Ry. .... | 54 | Stillmore, Ga. |
| Suffolk & Carolina Ry. .... | 75 | Suffolk, Va. |
| Surry, Sussex & Southampton Ry. ............... | 28 | Baltimore, Md. |
| Suwanee & San Pedro R. R. | 54 | Live Oak, Fla. |
| Sylvania Central Ry. ..... | 15 | Sylvania, Ga. |
| Tallulah Falls Ry. ........ | 28 | Cornelia, Ga. |
| Tavares & Gulf R. R. ..... | 35 | Clermont, Fla. |
| Tellico Ry. .............. | 24 | Athens, Ga. |
| Tennessee & Cumberland River R. R. ........... | 15 | Bear Spring, Tenn. |
| Tennessee & North Carolina R. R. ................. | 19 | Wheeling, W. Va. |
| Tennessee Central R. R. .. | 308 | Nashville, Tenn. |
| Tombigbee Valley Ry. ..... | 50 | Fairford, Ala. |
| Transylvania R. R. ....... | 42 | Brevard, N. C. |
| Union Springs & Northern Ry. .................. | 47 | Union Springs, Ala. |
| Valdosta Southern Ry. .... | 28 | Valdosta, Ga. |
| Valley R. R. ............ | 62 | Staunton, Va. (B. & O.) |
| Virginia & Southwestern Ry. .................. | 159 | Bristol, Va. |
| Virginia-Carolina Ry. ..... | 19 | Abingdon, Va. |
| Wadley & Mt. Vernon R. R. | 62 | Wadley, Ga. |
| Wadley & Mt. Vernon Extension R. R. ........ | 21 | Douglas, Ga. |
| *Washington Southern Ry. | 36 | Richmond, Va. (Richd.—Washn. Company) |

*Affiliated with those now identified with movement for revising plan.
†Now identified with movement for revising plan.

| Name of Carrier | Mileage Shown by the Official Guide | Location of General Office, Etc. |
|---|---|---|
| Wellington & Powellsville R. R. .................. | 24 | Edenton, N. C. |
| †Western Ry. of Alabama .. | 138 | Atlanta, Ga. |
| West Virginia Central & Pittsburg Ry. .......... | 211 | Baltimore, Md. |
| West Virginia Northern R. R. .................. | 11 | Tunnelton, W. Va. |
| *Wrightsville & Tennille R. R. .................. | 77 | Tennille, Ga. (Cent. of Ga.) |
| *Yazoo & Mississippi Valley R. R. .................. | 1,175 | Chicago, Ill. (Ill. Cent.) |
| *Yellow River R. R. ....... | 28 | Pensacola, Fla. (L. & N.) |
| Total ............ | 40,825 | |

## SUMMARY

Mileage of Carriers (as shown by the Official Guide):

| | | |
|---|---|---|
| Now identified with movement for revising plan, represented at meeting held October 28, 1904 ............ | 29,750 | |
| Affiliated with those now identified with movement for revising plan, but not represented at meeting held October 28, 1904 .............................. | 5,282 | 35,032 |
| Other—Not affiliated and not represented at meeting held October 28, 1904 .............................. | | 5,793 |
| Total .............................. | | 40,825 |

*Affiliated with those now identified with movement for revising plan.
†Now identified with movement for revising plan.

## Comments

The names of the respective carriers are omitted where the figures relate to their individual affairs. This has been done to avoid disclosing to one carrier something that might be regarded as of a private nature by another carrier, or the possibility of publicity.

In many cases, as is shown by Exhibit "B," the carriers authorize the local agents to pay claims of certain kinds up to certain amounts without making an investigation beyond the point necessary to determine that the claim is valid. The proposed plan is not intended to change this arrangement when the policy of the carrier has been established with reference to making payments through agents, but to make such investigation as in its judgment and according to its rules is now made before the settlement with the claimant. In doing this, however, the carrier should keep in mind that there must be sufficient investigation before the distribution is made against the other carriers interested, to know that the distribution is correct.

With good faith between the carriers, all the carriers could, under this plan, if they so desired, make settlement with all claimants as soon as the validity of each claim is established, without waiting for investigation by the other carrier or carriers in interest.

The forms to be used to facilitate the investigation between the carriers, and for the local investigation, may be arranged advantageously for use on the typewriter.

There will be an occasional inquiry sent to a carrier which the investigation will afterwards show not to have been necessary. These cases will, however, be very few in number.

The use of the form of inquiry, or base, provided for in the plan would vastly reduce the present labor expended in handling claim papers in offices, and mail matter on trains, at stations, and to and from offices. The superintendents, train-masters, yard-masters, station agents, clerks and others, who are now obliged to read through many pages of claim papers in order to ascertain the point at issue, will have before them, on one sheet of paper, all the information necessary for them to dispose of the matter at once. According to the present custom these officers are obliged to read pages upon pages of matters relating to the claim in general, but entirely irrelevant to the point necessary to be covered by any one particular carrier. It is impossible to estimate the enormous amount of time the proposed plan will save in this one respect alone.

The plan will completely dispose of practically all claims within a month or two. There will occasionally be an aggravated case that might call for a second inquiry concerning some remote matter pertinent to the investigation; but, from the examination already made of the claims in the different offices, it is believed that there will be very few such cases. The correspondence and the papers attached to the claims show that generally within a month practically every carrier investigates and determines all the points necessary to enable the settling carrier to settle with the claimant and make a distribution of the claim. The time consumed is in transmitting from one carrier to another and back again to the point of origin, including delay in handling; and after all the information necessary for the settlement of the claim has been drawn together, it goes back and forth to get into agreement on some point that has been evident to all the carriers in interest from the beginning, or on the distribution of the amount of the claim.

The provision for periodical settlements between the

carriers, included in the plan, obviates the necessity for each carrier's keeping individual ledger accounts of the distributions with each of the other carriers and is in harmony with what is known as the "Denver Plan." It is not intended that the statements upon which the periodical settlements are to be made by means of drafts shall preclude as frequent settlements as the carriers in interest may find mutually advantageous; on the other hand, it is meant to obligate the carriers to make settlement of all distributions made in any one month within 30 days after the close of that month.

The suggestion of a minimum amount below which interline claims shall not be distributed, arises from the fact that in a business transaction there is generally some point at which the amount is regarded as too small to justify the expenditure of labor and time entailed in making an exact settlement. It is difficult, if not impossible, to determine where this point is with reference to the settlement of interline claims; but it is thought that some amount not above $5 should be fixed as the minimum.

The records of seven of the carriers covering 13,229 overcharge and loss and damage claims were examined for the purpose of considering the question of the minimum. The average amount of these claims was $18.99.

It was found, as will be seen by Exhibit "E," that 11.4% of the total number of claims are for $1 and under, that they average 61 cents, and that the amount involved in these claims is .37% of the total amount of the claims; that 30.92% of the total number of claims are for $2.50 and under, that they average $1.32, and that the amount involved in these claims is 2.15% of the total amount of the claims; that 49.55% of the total number of claims are for $5 and under, that they average $2.21, and that the amount involved in these claims is 5.75% of the total amount of the claims; and that 66.61% of the total number of claims are for $10 and under, that they average $3.46, and that the amount involved in these claims is 12.13% of the total amount of the claims.

There is no way to determine what point, in fixing the minimum, would result in the greatest economy in both time and money under the plan proposed. In the case of $2.50 it would seem that nearly one-third of the interline claims will be disposed of without making the distribution between the carriers in interest, and that only 2% of the money involved will be affected; while in the case of $5 about one-half of the interline claims will be disposed of without making the distribution between the carriers in interest, and a little less than 6% of the amount involved will be affected. The amount to be fixed as a minimum is, therefore, a matter of policy rather than of deduction. It is believed that the minimum should not be fixed below $2.50 or above $5.

It is impossible to estimate the amount of work that will be done by the Arbitration Bureau. Its work will begin soon after the introduction of the plan and will increase gradually during the first year or so; but thereafter it should decrease. It is believed that an arbitrator with two able assistants, together affording the benefit of three minds when necessary to decide aggravated cases concerning which there may be disputes, and the necessary office help, will be sufficient at the beginning. Additions can, of course, be made from time to time, as may be found necessary. It is believed that the work of the Arbitration Bureau, will, in a few years, as the result of the educational process during this period, be reduced to a very small volume.

The settlement of interline claims being a mutual matter between the carriers, there appears to be no reason why the carriers in interest should not depend upon each other for the proper handling of the original papers and for the correct distribution of the amount paid; but if for any reason there should arise a doubt on the part of one or more of the carriers as to the good faith of another carrier, there is opportunity by this plan for examination of all the original papers in the same manner as at present, except that such examination will be after, instead of before, the settlement is made.

The present methods of handling claims by several of the carriers represented at the meeting on October 28, is shown by Exhibit "B."

A request was sent on November 3 to all of these carriers, and the responses received have been reproduced as an outline of the procedure in their respective offices. It may be said in a general way that there is a similarity in all the offices, the variation for the most part consisting of slightly different forms of records and varying grades of pay of investigators and clerks. The attitude of the carriers towards one another, generally, is to avoid payment rather than to facilitate settlement. This is attributable to the cumbersome system and unbusinesslike method of procedure. This is shown by the handling of certain claims outlined in Exhibit "C."

The interline claims paid by agents direct, together with those paid through the treasurer before authority is obtained from the connecting carrier, are in most cases charged to a suspense account, awaiting adjustment with the carriers in interest. These suspense accounts amount in several instances to many hundreds of thousands of dollars, and in most cases are continually increasing. There are, however, many interline claims left to be paid to the claimant after the carriers have agreed upon the distribution of the amount involved in the claim. In the suspense accounts large amounts are being accumulated that will ultimately have to be separated between actual assets, items collectible from connections, and amounts chargeable against freight earnings for overcharges and against operating expenses for loss and damage. In most cases the amount recoverable from connections is comparatively small. Some of the carriers have made provision by setting up estimated reserves for the amounts that are accumulating in the suspense accounts.

The work is divided in the different offices between overcharge claims, loss and damage claims, over, short, and damage reports, correspondence, files, and miscellaneous. Overcharge claims are usually settled with less difficulty and greater promptness than loss and damage claims.

The overcharge claims have been divided into three principal classes:

1. Rates and divisions;
2. Weights;
3. Classification.

The work in the offices, however, is usually divided between certain classes of overcharge claims, such as lumber, coal, and other important commodities, and sometimes between claims arising on shipments between important terminals.

The loss and damage claims are divided into four general classes:

1. Total loss, which is the shortage at destination of an entire shipment of one or more packages;

2. Concealed loss, where the package arrives at destination in apparent good order but where an examination of the contents reveals a deficiency in comparison with the contents shown by the original invoice;

3. Open damage, where the goods arrive at destination with the damage apparent;

4. Concealed damage, where the package arrives at

destination in apparent good order but where an examination of the contents reveals the damage.

The local claims, for both overcharge and loss and damage, that is to say claims on freight traffic having both its origin and destination on one carrier's line, are found to be settled with very little correspondence. In most cases these claims are disposed of, it is estimated, except in cases of dispute with the claimant, within a month.

The present methods of handling interline claims are shown in Exhibit "C." The cases described were selected from lots of 10 taken at random just as they were found being worked currently in five of the principal carriers' offices where examinations were made. Many more claims of a similar character could be exhibited out of those examined, but these few cases serve to illustrate the cumbersome methods now in use, the bad faith or inefficiency, or both, and to show that, worked upon the plan proposed, the investigation of any one of these claims would have been completed well within the month, and would have been ready for distribution by the settling line, except in one case—a large live stock claim—and that one within 2½ months. These cases may show a longer time involved in the settlement than many others, but they also show the advantage of the plan proposed in promptly disposing of the claims that now consume months and often years.

While these cases are a matter of serious concern to those in interest, to a casual reader they must appear ludicrous.

The aggregate number of claims received by eight of the carriers represented at the meeting is shown by Exhibit "D," also the division between local and interline claims. The figures show that about 28% of the claims received are local, and about 72% interline. The average cost of handling each claim is 28.33 cents. It is estimated that the amount of time consumed in handling an interline claim is from two to three times as much as in handling a local claim. There are submitted three calculations which show that if it takes two times as much time to handle an interline claim as a local claim, then it costs 32.96 cents, on the average, to handle an interline claim; if it takes 2½ times as much time to handle an interline claim as a local claim, then an interline claim costs 34.07 cents, on the average; if it takes three times as much time to handle an interline claim as a local claim, then an interline claim costs 34.86 cents, on the average.

It is assumed, for the purpose of this calculation, that it costs 34 cents each, on the average, to handle interline claims. It is shown by Exhibit "D" that out of a total of 560,316 interline claims received by eight of the carriers during the year ended June 30, 1904, 281,523 were received from other carriers, and that the remainder, 278,793, or a trifle less than one-half, originated on the lines of the respective carriers.

It is estimated that the cost in the claim offices of handling the interline claims will, under this plan, be reduced at least 50% of the present cost. This would make an aggregate annual saving to the eight carriers handling these 560,316 claims, of $95,253.72. The estimated cost is calculated on the basis of all the claims handled by the eight carriers referred to. The saving would, as a matter of course, be much larger for all the carriers in interest, and it would be relatively greater as the number of claims increases. The estimated saving would not be wholly applicable to the claims that involve the participation of carriers not parties to the plan; but whatever the cost of these claims may be, it must be more than offset by the expense now incurred in handling and rehandling the claim papers throughout the various departments of the carriers, other than the claim office; which expense, under the plan proposed, must necessarily be materially reduced. Besides this saving—and perhaps most important of all—will be the prompt settlement effected with the claimants, and the prompt adjustment between the carriers.

The names of the carriers whose lines lie in the southeastern territory, and their approximate mileage as given by the Official Guide of December, 1904, appear in Exhibit "F." This exhibit shows that out of a total of 40,825 miles, the carriers represented at the meeting of October 28 operate 29,750 miles, or 72.87% of the total mileage, and that their affiliated carriers operate 5,282 miles. This makes a total of 35,032 miles, or 85.81% of the total mileage, leaving approximately 5,793 miles of other carriers, besides the carriers that are not shown in Exhibit "F" operating small roads of less than 11 miles in length, and terminal, logging, coal, and private roads, being about 200 in number.

It is estimated that about 3,500 miles of the carriers represented at the meeting of October 28, 1904, lie outside of the southeastern territory.

Editorial Note: Mr. Sells wound up the year 1904, so to speak, with a report which stands as a monument to his ability as a public accountant. Such is his report, bearing the date of December 31, 1904, on a proposed plan for handling interline freight claims submitted to a committee of five railroad presidents representing the carriers in the southeastern territory. While this report was confidential at the time, so long a period has elapsed since it was rendered and so long has the plan been in use that it is considered no violation of confidence to publish it at this time. This view is concurred in by one of the foremost railroad men in the country.

The settlement of interline freight claims has been one

of the most perplexing problems of railway operation. When it requires 10 pages of 11-point type to describe the peregrinations of one claim, only moderate imagination is necessary to picture the amount of time, expense, annoyance, and dissatisfaction which was caused by the claim itself. Two and a half years were required to settle it, and 109 pieces of paper were attached to the claim. All this trouble was over a claim of $23.

The plan suggested for remedying this condition was adopted with slight modification after due consideration. It has been in operation ever since substantially as adopted, and it has been followed by practically all of the railroads throughout the United States. Although the saving effected is not possible of estimate, it is reasonable to assume that the amount thereof represents one of the important decreases in operating costs brought about through improvements in office routine.

This investigation was one of many which Mr. Sells directed involving a public interest. His professional work in connection with public utilities and with federal, state, county, and municipal investigations has won for him a distinguished position in the realm of accountancy.

# INDEX

# INDEX

G



H



I

## Q



## R

# *The History of Accounting*

*An Arno Press Collection*

Bennet[t], James [Arlington]. **The American System of Practical Book-Keeping** and Foster, B[enjamin] F[ranklin], **The Origin and Progress of Book-Keeping.** 1842/1852. Two vols. in one

Brief, Richard P., editor. **The Late Nineteenth Century Debate Over Depreciation, Capital and Income.** 1976

Brief, Richard P. **Nineteenth Century Capital Accounting and Business Investment.** 1976

Bruchey, Stuart W[eems]. **Robert Oliver and Mercantile Bookkeeping in the Early Nineteenth Century.** 1976

Church, A[lexander] Hamilton. **Production Factors in Cost Accounting and Works Management.** 1910

Cole, William Morse. **Accounts:** Their Construction and Interpretation for Business Men and Students of Affairs. 1908

Dicksee, Lawrence R[obert]. **Advanced Accounting.** 1903

Dicksee, Lawrence R[obert]. **Auditing:** A Practical Manual for Auditors. 1892

Dicksee, Lawrence R[obert]. **Auditing:** A Practical Manual for Auditors. Authorized American Edition, Edited by Robert H. Montgomery. 1905

Dicksee, Lawrence R[obert]. **Depreciation, Reserves, and Reserve Funds.** 1903

Dicksee, Lawrence R[obert] and Frank Tillyard. **Goodwill and Its Treatment in Accounts.** 1906

Folsom, E[zekiel] G[ilman]. **Folsom's Logical Bookkeeping:** The Logic of Accounts. 1873

Garcke, Emile and J[ohn] M[anger] Fells. **Factory Accounts, Their Principles and Practice.** 1893

Hatfield, Henry Rand. **Modern Accounting:** Its Principles and Some of its Problems. 1916

Kehl, Donald. **Corporate Dividends:** Legal and Accounting Problems Pertaining to Corporate Distributions. 1941

Leake, P[ercy] D[ewe]. **Depreciation and Wasting Assets and Their Treatment in Assessing Annual Profit and Loss.** 1912

Lisle, George. **Accounting in Theory and Practice.** 1900

Matheson, Ewing. **The Depreciation of Factories, Mines and Industrial Undertakings and Their Valuation.** 1893

Montgomery, Robert H. **Auditing Theory and Practice.** 1912

Norton, George Pepler. **Textile Manufacturers' Book-Keeping for the Counting House, Mill and Warehouse.** 1894

Paton, William A[ndrew] and Russell A[lger] Stevenson. **Principles of Accounting.** 1916

Pixley, Francis W[illiam]. **Auditors:** Their Duties and Responsibilities Under the Joint-Stock Companies Acts and the Friendly Societies and Industrial and Provident Societies Acts. 1881

Reiter, Prosper, Jr. **Profits, Dividends and the Law.** 1926

Scott, DR. **Theory of Accounts.** 1925

Scovell, Clinton H. **Interest as a Cost.** 1924

Sells, Elijah Watt. **The Natural Business Year and Thirteen Other Themes.** 1924

Soulé, Geo[rge]. **Soulé's New Science and Practice of Accounts.** 1903

Sprouse, Robert T[homas]. **The Effect of the Concept of the Corporation on Accounting.** 1976

Zeff, Stephen A., editor. **Asset Appreciation, Business Income and Price-Level Accounting: 1918-1935.** 1976